THE
GHOST
OF MY
FATHER

···

SCOTT BERKUN

The Ghost of My Father / Scott Berkun – 1st ed. Nov 2014
ISBN 978-0-9838731-2-9
Berkun Media, LLC

Dedicated to my nieces and nephews:
Jessica, Josh, Tara, Aaron, Aidan and Gavin

A portion of proceeds from this edition of this book
will be donated to Big Brothers Big Sisters of Puget Sound
and Big Brothers Big Sisters of America

"If the world were clear, art would not exist."
— Camus

"Write hard and clear about what hurts."
— Hemingway

CONTENTS

ONE

···

DOORS AND MEMORIES

When my mother cleaned out my father's car, she found tickets to a movie she'd never seen. They soon separated, and he moved away from our home on the east side of Queens, NYC. I was eight years old when it happened. No one recalls what the movie was, but it's strangely important to me now. If your family fell apart because of a movie, wouldn't that movie's name have significance? But no one remembers. She made other discoveries too – like lipstick on a cigarette and a woman's glove – but curiously, the only fact I recall is the tickets. And while the movie's name has been lost to time, my father's choices changed my family forever. He gave us our first experience of abandonment, of being left behind, and of feeling not good enough to be loved by someone who is supposed to love us the most.

Here and now I've discovered light in the past. I don't linger in my memories to justify sadness in the present.

Instead, I've found something glowing in those old thoughts I don't understand, and I'm compelled to uncover whatever is hiding there. This kind of search demands a return to hard times. There are clues in my past that may make sense only when I've seen them more than once.

I remember sad times during the separation. My mother often hid her despair in the basement, crying alone and smoking hidden cigarettes. My older siblings, Todd and Tracy, struggled as young teens to help her and help themselves. We all hid in our own corners of that house, forced to learn how to nurse our wounds. But I wasn't angry or sad when my father left. I barely knew him. I've realized now, as an adult, that I'm angry his leaving mattered so little in my life. I deserved a father involved enough that his departure, and his return, would mean something. All children deserve this, and I didn't get it. What does that signify for me now? I don't yet know. I have more memories to explore to find an answer.

I can admit for the first time that I come from a broken family. The events of this recent year of 2013, a wild story central to this book, have made this undeniable. Yet for most of my life I defended my family as a matter of principle. We all want to feel pride in our families, and that's what makes dysfunction common. We feel ashamed to criticize our own blood in front of outsiders. And we refuse to let light shine in to our private feelings, afraid of how we'll feel when our truths are revealed. It's a scary thing to know each other for who we are rather than for who we want each other to be.

Maybe I was sad back then, but I certainly didn't know it. I was proud of my family simply because I needed to be someone who was proud of their family. I considered myself happy, happier than my parents or my siblings. I had friends, and I played sports I loved, and that was enough. But maybe my family saw the same sadness in me that I saw in them.

It was only later, in my twenties, that I noticed the effects the sad seed of those early years had planted. Why did I love to argue? Why did I hate to lose? Why did I share so little with people I was close with? After college I moved away and finally had the distance to examine myself, who I really was and why I'd grown up the way I had. I realized becoming an adult demanded I recognize what I needed and hadn't received, or what had been forced upon me that hurt me. All adults in age have feelings about the past they need to explore before they can be adults emotionally. Even if I'd had superhero parents, I'd still have had an imperfect childhood with issues and questions I'd need to explore. A perfect family, if such a thing exists, denies children experience with imperfection, something they will encounter in every relationship they have, including the one they have with themselves.

If I suffer from denial, it's my wishful belief there are facts hidden in my old memories, facts imbued with powers to explain the unexplainable. My family is an enigma to me, and I don't want it to be. I know magic doesn't exist, but for some things, knowing is not enough. I have faith that even if I fail to explain the past, by trying I will know myself better, an achievement worth the hard work the search demands.

I'm forty-two now, a decade older than my parents were when they separated. I have the life experience to try to understand what they did and why. My mother and father have generously granted intimate conversations, with answers of a kind many people only offer their therapists, if to anyone at all. Who was this other woman? Why, Father, did you leave? Why did you return? Why, Mom, did you take him back three years later? My parents raised a brave child and now endure the curse of an all-too-curious adult, one who happens to write. But my goal is not revenge: my ambition is wisdom. Questions beget questions, and my parents answered them all. That is, all the answers they could remember and the questions I could think to ask.

Some memories we love to share with other people. We tell the stories of how we met a friend or spouse hundreds of times, polishing the details with each telling. Other memories we review privately, again and again, from different angles, at different speeds, and with different questions. They hold a story we compulsively remember, like a reflex of the mind. We don't consciously choose to recall them; instead, they take us over like a force of nature. Marcel Proust called these involuntary memories. He famously told a story of how one bite of a madeleine cookie transported him to another place and time with an intensity beyond the experience of normal recollections. He believed involuntary memories tell us more about ourselves than the ones we choose to recall.

There is one memory of my father that I've entertained in the theater of my mind many times. One day, during the separation, my father visited the house. I was playing in my room, and as no one else was around, I had to go down the stairs to answer the door. I thought maybe it was my friend Brad who lived across the street or one of my brother Todd's friends who was looking for someone to join in a basketball game. I skipped down the long staircase, crossed the hall, and unlocked the door, pulling it open with my right hand. The white storm door on the outside remained closed, and I looked up through its window to see who was there. I was surprised to see my father's eyes looking down at me.

He was like a god. He was the strongest, smartest, scariest person I knew. I believed then that he knew everything, even though he knew little about me. And with the recent separation, I didn't know if he was on my side or another. It must have been the first time he visited the house since the separation. He didn't smile when he saw me that day. But I wasn't surprised that he didn't smile. He didn't smile often, not back then.

I was the same age then that my nephew Joshua is now. When I look at Joshua, with his sweet smile and bushy hair, I imagine he looks something like what I must have looked like to my father. But unlike my nephew, who is warm with confidence, I was scared that day. I didn't smile when I saw my father. My small hands struggled to open the storm door, the kind with the black air pump that made quiet squeaking sounds when it slowly closed, as if by magic, on its own. I didn't know what to do. Was I supposed to let my father in? What were the rules when a parent moves away? No one had told me. I felt certain I was going to do something wrong, but I had often felt that way around him. He was my father, so I waited for him to offer something, to set the tone or lead the way, but he offered nothing. I said, "What do you want?", as it was the only thing I could think to say. Then I went upstairs to tell my mother he was here. I left my father on the porch, with the sputtering sounds of that storm door, little bursts of air releasing as it closed, slowly shutting him out behind me. After I found my mother, I went back to my room. I didn't see my father again that day, as he left without finding me to say goodbye.

When it happened it meant nothing. I didn't think about it the next day or the next week. As strange as it might have been to greet my father at the door of his own house, it seemed normal then. The innocence of childhood hinges on its lack of context. When we are young, we don't know how one experience compares to others, since we've had so few of them. It's only when we're older that we can look back and understand what happened. We can project backward how we might have felt if we weren't so innocent. And that day at the door grows in power each time it comes to my mind.

I've learned that moment at the door stands out today in my father's mind too. He told me recently that the very same memory had stuck with him over these decades just like it had with me. He had somehow expected a warm welcome from the family he left and had been disappointed. I can see how it must have been strange to wait on the cement porch of his own home, standing by the white railings, railings he'd paid for and painted himself. But what he has never understood was I looked to him for how to behave. I was the child. I hadn't put him on that side of the door, outside his own house; he had put himself there. And he had put me on the inside of that house, a house without a father, a house of lost people, a house where I'd have to answer the door when my father knocked and confront him at the door to his home. I realize now we were two children at that door, only I was his son.

On occasional Sundays during the separation, my father drove to the house to take me out for the afternoon. Sometimes Todd, the oldest, or Tracy, our middle sister, would come along. But in my memory, inexplicably, it's only the two of us: my father Howard and me. Those afternoons were the closest we had to a functioning relationship, as broken as it was. Like being sentenced to do community service, we at least had a commitment to show up at a set time and place and honored it. Many children don't get even that much from their fathers, a sad fact I've considered many times. But three years later, when my parents reunited and he moved back in, our outings ended. There was no discussion about it; the offers to do things together stopped coming. I've tried to find other memories, other stories of the two of us sharing something, but there are few to find – just a handful of lost afternoons during difficult years.

The outings were sad affairs: a depressed man in crisis and the confused, quiet little boy I was around him. I have gray memories of miniature golf at the place in Douglaston I'd been to dozens of times for elementary school birthday parties. It seemed so fun to go there with friends, making silly faces to distract each other from our turns, or sharing tips on how to beat the tougher holes, but being there with my father was absent of easy joy. On other days, we went to matinee movies, stopping for pizza on the way there. But since we didn't have any shared interests, these afternoons were filled with silence. There hadn't been much of a relationship before the separation, and even if there had been, separations and divorces strain even the healthiest ones.

I loved baseball at the time, and it was my father's favorite sport, but even that wasn't enough to connect us. We went to one game at Yankee Stadium, but all I recall is my surprise when he yelled from the stands at the umpire. Standing tall in the seat next to me, he cupped his hands over his mouth and screamed with the madness of the crowd. It shocked me to see him yell so intensely about something so distant while I sat so close. I didn't want him to see my fear, so I hid it. I behaved the way I thought I was supposed to and did nothing more. It's no surprise neither of us had fun on these outings. And neither of us knew how to change how it was.

Week after week we'd never address the one true thing we shared: our disappointment. For misery to love company, everyone has to admit they're miserable, which suggests that a person who can't admit to being miserable will always be alone (and always miserable too). That's part of the mystery of my father: I'm not sure he knew then, or now, when he was miserable or not. The tiny little circuit of emotional self-awareness most people have never worked well for him. He couldn't calibrate how these outings should compare to other outings we'd been on before the affair, since few had occurred. The affair, and the separation, was what forced the motivation to make deliberate plans to see me at all.

On the drive back from many of these outings, we'd speed across the Belt Parkway, riding through Brooklyn toward the house in Bay Terrace, Queens. He liked to drive fast, and I remember the brick overpasses flying overhead and the empty trees of winter hovering over rows of navy blue houses. And I'd stare out the window, watching the world fly by, not saying anything. The filmstrip memory of that drive has played forever in my mind. Endless car rides in silence, but not alone.

When the quiet went on too long, he'd say, almost sweetly, "A penny for your thoughts," to which I never had an answer. I didn't have any thoughts. I didn't know what was going on. I feared asking him a serious question would only make him angry. Keeping quiet was safe. I wasn't in control and had little influence on what was happening. Those car rides linger so strongly in my memory because I was, as all kids are, along for the ride. The helplessness of those car rides echoed the helplessness of being a child in that family.

My father had the sharpest of wits, but he used it to cut people down, especially the people closest to him. Todd once came home from a little league baseball game, and Howard asked him how it went. Todd said, "I got two walks," a respectable but modest achievement. Our father replied, "My grandmother can walk" and said nothing more. My siblings and I all have inventories of these stories, innocent moments transformed into surprise attacks. The implicit message to my brother was you are not good enough, and your father, who is telling you that you are not good enough, is not going to help you become good.

Children can only be victims in these encounters. But as an adult, it's easy to see the wider picture: Why wasn't my father at the game to see for himself? Why wasn't he offering to teach Todd to hit better or looking for something, anything, positive to say to his oldest son? There was plenty of responsibility my father could have taken if he wanted it, but he didn't. He mastered wounding us just enough that we'd leave the conversations as quickly as we could. This was an outcome my father, without fully understanding why, found desirable. He didn't want to give much, or didn't have much to give, and these barbs and jabs were an easy way to ensure the distance remained.

As the youngest, I had the easiest time avoiding him. I benefited from watching how Todd, Tracy, and my mother were wounded by his words. I kept my distance, and if my mother didn't initiate something for me and my father to do together, he rarely did. She'd tell me to go help him paint the front railing or work with him on the car in the garage. When I did, I found him perfectly pleasant. Often he was patient in teaching me what there was to learn, like how to replace a spark plug or use a screwdriver. But he never said much. It didn't seem to matter if I was there or not. I kept quiet, did what was required, and faded away when my tasks were done. That was the pattern I learned during the separation, and I didn't see the need for a better one when the separation ended. I learned not to ask him for advice, not to ask him for anything. I shared the house with my father, but not my life.

By the time I was a senior in high school, I was desperate to leave Queens and go out into the world on my own. I went away to college and was proud, given the struggles I had, to graduate on time. But my graduation day was depressing, as despite how hard I'd worked to find a job and start my life, I had no real prospects ahead of me. I'd watched many of my friends accept job offers long before graduation. Despite dozens of job interviews, numerous career counseling sessions, and reading many books on finding work, I still had no offers. By June of 1994, I had two choices. I could either move back in with my parents, which I saw as a failure, or I could stay in my girlfriend Jill's apartment, buying time to figure out what I was going to do. It was an easy decision, and I stayed with Jill.

I also decided to ask my father for advice. I wasn't close with my uncles or aunts. I didn't know any adults who I thought could help. I chose my father, as he was the only person in my life who had experience with the working world. It took weeks to work up the courage. I hadn't asked him for advice on anything in years, certainly nothing that made me feel as vulnerable as this did. I felt like a failure and was desperate. I decided to show him my resume the next time I drove home from Jill's Pittsburgh apartment to visit for the weekend.

He was in his office on the first floor of the house, a room that had been Todd's bedroom before he moved out after college. I walked down the stairs, stairs I'd skipped down thousands of times to greet friends at the door or to hang out with my brother. This time was different, and I thought about turning around on every step. I noticed the new fish tank outside his door, with glass three feet wide, filled with quiet little creatures he tended to every day. I looked just past the tank to the front door, and I realized I could just keep going. I didn't have to stop. I could go on out the door and walk away. But I didn't walk away. My desperation for a job outweighed whatever pride I had left in not asking my father for help.

His door was open, and I knocked. I said, "Hey Dad, do you have a minute?" He was at his desk, which faced the door, typing away on his computer. He nodded yes, without taking his eyes off the computer screen. I could see the blue glare of the stock trading program he used reflecting in his glasses. He had a TV behind the computer monitor that always had one of the business networks playing, a stock ticker running across the bottom. He followed that ticker in spare moments when he thought no one noticed his attention wasn't on them, but I usually did. I collected myself and told him why I'd come to talk.

"Could you look at my resume and tell me what you think?" I asked and offered the resume to him.

He reached across the desk and took it from my hand. Without looking up, he began his examination. He shook his head ever so slightly, as if disappointed I'd make mistakes as obvious as he thought they were. In hindsight the resume was in fact quite good. I still have a copy of it.

"Why did you put this here? It should be further down," he said. He added, with an expression of mild distaste like what one would make after drinking an old cup of coffee, "The dates should be on the right, not on the left."

I'd rewritten and revised it hundreds of times during my desperate senior year. I'm sure I had had versions with all of the suggestions he made but had reversed them in the desperate hope young graduates have that the resume holds magical job-finding powers. Of course a resume, at best, only gets you in the door. But I couldn't know that then. Perhaps he could have, but his need to dismiss what I'd shown him was more important.

When I'd handed him the resume, I'd forgotten something about myself I still struggle to remember. Just because I needed his help enough to ask for it didn't change that he was always the first source of doubt in my life. Like putting your hand in the river and expecting not to get wet, bringing ideas to him was certain only to make me feel worse about whatever it was. He was intelligent and creative in finding negative things to say about anything. There was not, and hadn't been, any mention of how hard I'd been working to find a job. Or how impressive it was to graduate on time, given I'd transferred between three colleges along the way. Perhaps he didn't know any of this, but he didn't ask.

The resume encounter hurt me in an old way, a wound I'd been trying to avoid most of my young life. I felt far worse after talking to him than before, and while sitting there, I realized I'd made a mistake. This was the same man I'd seen do this to everyone in the family, and I was stupid enough to invite more of it on myself.

But when the conversation ended, something new happened, something I didn't expect. For all my life, I'd absorbed those jabs and criticisms. I'd never thought to challenge him, at least not directly. This time a voice inside me spoke up, and I don't know where it came from. I said, "Thanks for the feedback. But did you have to be so mean about it?" It was the first time in my life I'd given him adult commentary on his behavior instead of the passive-aggressive sarcasm of a teenager. It surprised him. He looked at me directly, more directly than he had during the rest of the conversation. This was new, I thought. Something good might happen here.

But then he asked, in his classic fashion: "What do you want me to do? Butter it up for you?"

I sighed, and with that breath, whatever hope I'd had disappeared. He didn't see me as a person with feelings, and I didn't know how to show him otherwise. The old wound, the one I didn't know how to defend, had been punched again, and this time I'd invited it. I retreated into the familiar loop of feeling weak for asking for help and feeling worse for knowing I was still a failure.

I look back at this memory, as a man of my own, and want to yell at him: "Whose side are you on?" From this vantage point in time, there was no evidence for assuming my father was on mine. I was bright and ambitious, more than my siblings had been at that age, but I was left to figure that out on my own. Like all children, I took the wounds of that day and all days like it to be a reflection of something lacking in myself – something my father wouldn't even care to take the time to explain.

I couldn't know it then, but fathers are our templates for all men. The same unresolved issues and fears I had of my father I had of most men in my life. I never went to office hours or to see tutors in college, even when I desperately needed guidance. I'd tough it out all on my own, making myself sick in the fight to do everything alone. Our bodies pay the price for the emotions we ignore. It's no surprise to me now that I was sick enough to be hospitalized once a year, around final exams, throughout college. It was far more painful to imagine arriving at a professor's desk with only confusion and broken thoughts than any alternative. I didn't want strangers to tear me down the way my father had. I denied it all, a slave to my own invented idea of a man as someone who didn't need help. And I had the hubris of youth, believing everyone was weak if they didn't want to be as self-reliant as I thought I was.

We all suffer wounds in our childhoods. We do what we have to do to protect ourselves, but we forget when we become adults that the armor made to survive our youth no longer serves us. It's for use in the last war, the struggles of childhood, not the war or the peace of the present and the future. Keeping that armor keeps us immature. We can't grow with it on. Yet removing it is painful. Taking it off means our true selves will be revealed. Revelations divide who we were in the past from who we want to be in the future, and we can't predict where that division will take us. It can put us at odds with our own family and friends, as tribes prefer to stay with patterns of the past. Most people convince themselves that removing their armor is work they don't need to do. And their families, complicit in the same denial, reward the defense of the status quo, ensuring the same wounds, the same armor, and the same ghosts will be passed on to the next generation and the next.

Today I can see, looking back at those early years, how miserable my father was. I feel sad for him. He was younger and far more lost, even on the day I showed him my resume, than I've ever been. He simply had nothing to give to me or anyone else. His own father had given him even less to work with than he was giving me. I imagine my father's life was a disappointment to him. He had imagined an impossible greatness for himself in wealth that he never achieved. His refuge for as long as I lived in that house was escape: the escape of work, the escape of the racetrack, and the escape of the blackjack table. What I experienced wasn't aimed directly at me, even though as a child I felt it was. He simply knew no other way to be, and he didn't possess the courage or motivation to find a way. He was unknowingly passing on his worst limitations: to deal privately with his wounds, to put himself first, and to deny and repress the expression of love. Like many young parents, he never noticed that for all of his anger at his own upbringing, he was passing on many of the mistakes his parents had passed on to him.

When I look back at those memories, there's a gift I wish I could give the younger version of me: a handwritten note from the future that says, simply, *This sucks, but it's not you.* I wish my brother, sister, mother, or even a stranger on the street had pulled me aside and whispered, slowly and lovingly, a poem of context into my young ear. Something I might not understand in the moment but that I'd play with in daydreams. But perhaps no poem has this kind of power, as I desperately wanted to be a part of my family, and any secret message that questioned the order of things wouldn't have been believed, at least not at first. But maybe the memory of that message would have helped me connect the dots earlier in life and with less of a price to pay.

There is only one outing with my father during the separation that I recall where Tracy and Todd came along. My father took us to VIP Pizza on Bell Boulevard, one of his favorite places in Bayside. It was on a long row of restaurants and bars, built up around the Long Island Railroad station, a station I'd use years later as a teenager to get to Manhattan when I had the money to upgrade from the local 7 subway train. VIP Pizza was a tiny place, with just a long counter in the front and a handful of tables in the back. It had all the trappings from the NYC pizza place kit: a neon sign out front, a two-level glass case showing the latest pizzas near the cash register, and short Italian-looking men with well-combed hair in white kitchen overalls slinging pizza and sodas all day long.

When our pizza was ready, we went to an empty table and sat down to eat. We'd been there many times before, but this time something was strange. My brother Todd refused to sit down. He stood by the wall near us and looked away into the distance. He leaned on his hands, which were behind him touching the wall: it was like they were handcuffed together, and he was hiding them from view. I, on the other hand, was hungry and excited. I still didn't like cheese and would pull it off the slices before I ate them, to the dismay of most cheese-loving pizza place patrons. But I did it anyway, and my family knew about it and didn't even complain anymore.

Sitting there, waiting to eat, there was nothing on my mind except the pleasure of folding that first slice, imagining the triangled tip flopping just slightly as I put it into my mouth. The crust felt right in my hand, and I held the pizza with a napkin in my palm to catch the grease that slides down when pizza is held properly, something my father had taught me. But when I noticed Todd wasn't sitting down, I was surprised. I couldn't imagine what was wrong. We were a family, mostly together, about to share a meal at a familiar place. We all loved to eat pizza. My brother had seemed fine earlier that day and even in the car on the drive to the restaurant.

My father noticed and asked Todd to sit. Todd refused by silently shaking his head. My father asked him again, pointing to the empty chair, but Todd did not give in. My father stared at Todd for a long moment and then, without another word, he gave up and started eating. Tracy began to eat too. It was just me who was too uncomfortable with Todd's discomfort. When I realized no one else cared, the alarm in me grew louder. It felt awkward to say anything, but I worked up the courage to ask, "Todd, what's wrong?" He didn't answer. He just shook his head at me, tears in his eyes. He shook his head as if to wave me off, to assure me that I shouldn't be worried, but I was. I didn't understand.

I looked to my father and sister who were already eating, and they didn't seem troubled at all. Unsure of myself, I tried to follow along with my father and go ahead and eat, but I didn't enjoy that meal. The only thing on my mind was Todd and my confusion. There was a lie at that table, a lie I didn't understand. Was Todd angry at something? Was he wrong for standing? It was an unresolved moment, one of hundreds our family would have. I'd never felt anything like it before, but I'd feel it again many times before I left that house.

Todd never came on another outing. Standing had been his silent protest against my father, a message Howard didn't understand, or worse, didn't care to answer. But my brother had planted a seed for me. The silent drama between his feelings and my father's indifference never resolved itself. Like an act of civil disobedience, his silence spoke louder than any dramatic outburst could have. Todd couldn't have known it then, but I heard the message intended for my father, and it has stayed with me for more than thirty years.

This is the surprise of memory. We don't know what of our experiences today will matter most in our future. We don't know what choices we make will last the longest in the minds of those closest to us. Powerful memories are a surprise, and the past is always alive, bringing different stories from our history back to us depending on what happens in the present.

There are happier memories from my early years, but they're hard to remember now. The reason why is in the summer of 2012 I learned that, at the age of seventy, my father was having another affair. Thirty years after the first one, my father put his family in crisis again. From the moment I learned the news, my thoughts returned to the sad, tired memories I've shared so far in this book. They hadn't been on my mind often, not for many years. Now they've risen again, like the ghosts of sad creatures that died long ago, haunting me because they want to find peace but can't. The recent news has changed the shape of these recollections so that no matter how I try, they never fit together the way I want them to.

It is curious, perhaps even strange, that the choices of my father would impact me so profoundly at forty years old. It surprised me too. I didn't decide in a moment of deep thought that I should dedicate countless hours to thinking, yet again, about my childhood. I didn't have any rational motivations. I was driven to do it, compelled by some of the oldest feelings I have about who I am. Maybe everyone, no matter how well adjusted, successful, and self-aware, has something about themselves they struggle their whole lives to fully understand. Or maybe life takes an unexpected turn, raising doubts about what had been the solid foundations of the past.

Memory is dubious because the way we perceive the world is dubious. We have blind spots, cognitive biases, and suffer from optical illusions. Our brains invent things to fill the gaps, but we have no awareness of their handiwork. Eyewitness testimony, even testimony given moments after a robbery or a car accident, is highly unreliable. And even when it's accurate, each person's attention focuses on different things, noticing and recalling only parts of what happened. Perhaps the reason I remember only the ticket stub my mother found in my father's car is because I've always had a deep love for movies, nostalgia for the printed tickets that grant you admission, and little interest in cigarettes or gloves.

We think of memory as if it were a filmstrip, photographic in detail, but this is a convenient fantasy. Each memory is stored as fragments strewn across different parts of our brains. Every time a memory is recalled, those fragments come together slightly differently. And the only way to remember certain memories is to repeat a condition present when the memory happened, which explains Proust's magical madeleines. This is why the scent of the ocean, or a stroll through an old neighborhood, brings back clear recollections of events that haven't crossed our mind in decades. It's the unifying link that pulls together all of the pieces.

Contrary to our deepest instincts, our memories of specific events change each time we remember them – at least that's what I remember from reading books about memory. Certain details are amplified, while others are diminished. Despite our false confidence that our strongest memories are the most accurate, there's increasing evidence the opposite is true. Abigail Lewis wrote that the past is every bit as unpredictable as the future, and she meant that depending on what happens to us in the present, surprises surface in the past. The very notion of the past shifts for each of us depending on our present. Some memories come into focus, and others fade away. Our minds add meaning to events that seemed meaningless a decade ago when they occurred, and take meaning away from events that seemed important when they happened. History lives on with us, shifting and twisting through time. And we change the stories in small ways as we tell them, shaping them to fit who we wish we were or who we want to be.

Memory is a kludge, but it's all we have for our thoughts – all we have except for writing. We can write down on any day what happened, and those words will persist exactly as we wrote them in ways we know our memories do not. Keeping a diary might just be the sanest thing we can do. But most of us push on through our days with the false certainty that we know what we think we know. We are all like Leonard Shelby, the main character from the film *Memento*, stumbling through life with misplaced faith in our memories, our minds, and our identities. This notion of memory is important. It will come up many times in this book, so please remember it, if you can.

The meaning of my past changed on an innocent day in the summer of 2012. I was visiting my parents' home in Connecticut, where they'd moved, with my sister, many years earlier. My brother also lived just a few miles away. I'd been visiting all of them once a year, for nearly twenty years, since I moved away to Seattle after college. My mother had picked me up at Todd's place, and she was going to drive me back to her house so we could have dinner together with my father. It was an ordinary day of me visiting my family, catching up and reconnecting.

I've always felt close to my mother, even when we didn't talk for long stretches of time. Her warmth and ability to share her feelings explain much of who I am, although it took me the better part of my life to recognize this was true. She could laugh and cry about almost anything, finding humor in even the darkest of times, a trait I am proud to share. But like I was with everyone in my family, I often felt at a distance from her. When my parents reunited, I was eleven years old and wanted to become a man, which I defined as not needing my mother for much of anything. I thought that's what a man was: someone who didn't need anyone else, certainly not their mother. Despite my confused masculine ambitions, she was the parent I trusted most and knew best, a beacon of warmth, openness, and positive emotions throughout my childhood.

As we walked to her car, she made a joke about her age. "I better drive, as who knows how much longer you'll trust me with your life."

We both laughed. We sat down and closed the doors, but before she put the car in gear, she grabbed my left hand. She didn't look at me; instead, her attention was out in the distance through the windshield. She told me she had something important to say. I said, "Sure, I'm happy to listen." She said she wasn't sure who else to talk to. The night before, I'd shared with her and my father some struggles in my own marriage, and she said hearing me talk about it inspired her to now share in kind. "Happy to help if I can," I said, not realizing how much of my world was about to change.

She told me Howard had been acting strange since his return from a recent trip to Australia – a trip he'd taken alone. I was rarely a confidant of either parent, but I'd had many conversations in my life with her that were very personal. Even so, this conversation was unusual. I didn't remember having one that started quite this way, which made me feel good at the time. I told her I was certain this moment was okay. I gave her a loving smile and told her I was genuinely glad to listen and help if I could. I didn't understand what she was trying to say or what was happening, but I wasn't afraid.

Sitting in the car, Mom thanked me for being willing to listen. She told me Howard had been back from Australia for weeks but hadn't shared much about the trip. He hadn't responded to most of her emails while he had been away either. Immediately I imagined he was having another affair. The wheels in my brain went into overdrive with a thousand questions, thoughts, and memories, and I had to concentrate to listen to what she was saying.

As the wheels slowed down in my mind, my heart broke for her. She was still telling me the facts she'd collected, but I know men are simple creatures. There are only so many reasons for silence, even for a man like him. Whatever the truth was, how sad for her to have a partner for fifty years, to share a lifetime together, and then have these doubts haunt her mind. As a family, we had barely survived his first affair, and I couldn't imagine doing it again even though all of us children were now adults. But I kept myself together and listened on. I said simple things. I told her I loved her. I told her I'd help her figure it out.

When she finished, I gave her advice she'd once given me. I told her she needed to figure out who she could lean on. Who was her support team? Who were her true friends? If she was right about my father, she would need to depend on those friends heavily and quickly. The sooner she knew who her real friends were, the better. She was close with her sister and had some friends in Connecticut. I recommended she reach out to them immediately. She liked my advice and cried in that way mothers cry when they feel loved. She thanked me and began to drive us home to their house where Howard was waiting for us. When we fell into silence, I asked a question.

"Are we still going out to dinner with Dad tonight?"

She said, "Of course. Why wouldn't we?"

Why wouldn't we indeed. Apparently this situation was only strange to me. I was along for the ride yet again.

I didn't realize in that moment in the car that I was about to learn an important truth: families are linked together forever. I was brazen enough to think that my independence, being the most distant child from the family, made me safe from what my mother had shared. But if we pull hard on one end of a chain, the other end is pulled as well, no matter how far apart the two ends are. These chains can be used for good, to support us in tough times, but they're just as strong when working against us. All things can be good or bad depending on how they're used. The links to our family may have been well buried by our own careful hands years ago, but when a powerful force suddenly pulls hard on the chains, we're thrown down to the ground. And in the first moment when we turn over in shock, disoriented and angry, with pain in our side and dirt in our mouth, we remember that the old emotions never go away completely. We only have one father and one mother for as long as we live.

But I didn't know that then in the car. I didn't make this realization during that entire familial visit, even as it reached otherworldly levels of strangeness. Instead, I thought to myself, "How interesting." I'd never have guessed at my parents' age that anything like this could happen. I like to think of myself as an adventurous man, and in the mischievous cave in my soul where my writer's mind lives, I was excited by this turn of events. I had no idea where it would lead, but I sensed a good story might be found if I followed along. So I did. I said to myself, "I'm a very independent and self-aware adult," putting convenient faith in the notion that this kept me safe from my feelings about the past.

It's easy, as a child, to take what parents provide for granted. It's only as an adult I see how many things my mother and father gave to me, things I hadn't earned. The basement of the house in Queens where I grew up was one of my favorite places in the world. My family moved into the Bay Terrace neighborhood just as it was being finished, and I was born at Long Island Jewish Hospital soon after my family moved in. I remember, in my teens, seeing a photo of our street before any of the houses were finished, endless rows of wood frames and bare streets out to the horizon. Buying that house was good fortune for my family. The value of that small house grew as I did, and its value helped make my dream of going to college possible.

From that house I walked the half-mile every day to P.S. 169, my elementary school, and from there I ran with my friends to Jack's Pizza & Pasta for lunch. We'd race through the neighborhood to see who could run the fastest and reserve the best seats for their favorite friends. As a teenager, I'd make the same walks late at night to Peter Pan, the local video arcade a few stores down from Jack's. I lived a young life of independence because of that house, and that neighborhood, a freedom children today couldn't imagine. And when my friends came over for birthday parties or for after-school play, we'd stay down in that basement, the space my father had built.

He had put in the walls himself and finished the room with the fake wood paneling with black borders, the height of style in 1975. By the time I was six years old, the basement was furnished with a big black couch, a record player, and a green Ping-Pong table. I don't remember when my father bought that table, but I'm glad he did. Todd and I spent hundreds of hours in epic best-of-seven games to see who would be the house champion, and I'd storm up the stairs in a fury every time I lost, which was most of the time. I was a horrible loser, angry and bitter, but I didn't give up. Eventually I learned from those games both how to win and how to lose.

While I don't remember ever playing Ping-Pong with my father, Todd has told me the whole thing was my father's idea. He bought the table with my siblings and me in mind and encouraged us to play. It was my father who also chose to fit a tiny basketball court into the backyard, an area so small I sometimes had to shoot while standing on one foot, forced to lean over the air conditioning fan mounted on the ground. I'd spend most of my waking hours as a teenager on basketball courts, or wishing I was. I loved living in that house, and

I loved that basement. I know those are things my father gave to me. He worked hard in his way to make that house a home, and in my memory it was. But I find it hard now to see him with us in that house. I can't recall him having fun with us in the basement or even watching Todd and me play. I don't recall him keeping score or cheering us on. There are just shadows now when I look inside these memories for him. I sense him in the corner, a shadowy force of sadness, distant and alone, looking down with disapproving eyes on everything and everyone.

I remember my father teaching me how to play baseball, or at least I can't imagine that he didn't. Who else would I have learned from? Even as a young boy, I knew baseball was one of my father's great loves, though he rarely played. In my lifetime I've only seen him take the field once: at a softball game with his co-workers while I was in junior high school. He often spoke fondly of playing as a kid and bragged about how talented he was. I often asked him why he hadn't played for his high school or why he hadn't even tried out for the team. He never gave a good answer. The things he loved scared him somehow. Even baseball, our biggest chance to connect back then, was a lost cause. The only memento I have from the years I played in little league is a game ball I earned. There are no photos or scrapbooks.

At the one game I remember him watching, he sat in a folding chair far in the distance, past the dugouts and stands, his eyes hidden behind sunglasses. During that game I knew he was there, in the distance, and that meant something, but not as much as encouragement or pointers on how to play better might have. People can be physically present and emotionally far away simultaneously, and that's often what I felt from him when he was around.

My father's trip to Australia was a big surprise, as he'd never expressed much interest in travel. He was a very smart man, but plagued by ignorance, and arrogant about that ignorance. Once, in a recent argument about world politics, he yelled at me, "Why do I need to go to France to understand the French? I know all I need to know!" In a certain frame of mind he wouldn't listen to anyone, and that was perhaps his favorite frame. He could bully and out-debate everyone around him, and he relied on those abilities to win arguments even when he had little knowledge of the subject, or even more dangerous, when he knew for certain he was wrong.

Once every few years he'd get an idea for travel in his mind. He talked once of going to Lithuania and Romania to see where our ancestors had come from. Another notion was to visit London and Paris to learn something of world history firsthand. I thought these were great ideas, and I encouraged him to go. I told him about the amazing treasures in the British Museum, how he could see an original copy of the Magna Carta, something that would appeal to his vast knowledge of history and geography. But he'd always find ways to talk himself out of these trips. His fears would use his intelligence to invent excuses not to go.

He eventually decided Lithuania and Romania were not worthy destinations. His rationalization was that although our Jewish ancestors had lived there for generations, being Jewish meant they had not been treated as citizens there, which made the locations unworthy of visiting. I never understood this, as I'd love to go to these places. Either our family had lived somewhere for a century, or they had not. These places were unique regardless of how our family had been treated there, but I didn't argue with him; I knew it was a waste of time to try. His fears were in command, and facts are useless against someone in denial of their fears. After September 11, traveling by plane was out of the question, as he believed it was too dangerous, eliminating Europe and the rest of the planet as well. He was close to being the better man some part of him wanted to be, but the rest of him held tightly to the little world he knew. No one on this planet, not even his wife or his children, could shake his grip, or so I had thought.

Most of what I've known of my father's thoughts was told to me by my mother. When he lost his job while I was in college, I learned of it from her. She also told me when there was news of his brother or mother. She was his press secretary to the family, and I thought nothing of it, as she was easier to talk to than he was. She signed my report cards and gave me my allowance. And she loved to feel central to the family, relishing the role of queen of information. When Mom told me during the fall of 2011 that he was planning a trip to Australia, I was surprised, but not because she was the one who told me instead of him.

She explained that his turning seventy years old affected him deeply. This was the age his father had died. She supported the trip and told me it was a way for him to explore his life. I soon emailed him to say I was proud of him for going. I'd been to Australia several times and offered him my advice. I'd also been proud of him recently for listening to new music. He'd discovered rap and hip-hop, replacing Todd as the primary family member I'd exchange music recommendations with. For the first time in a long time, there were new things in him I admired. I hoped when I was his age I was brave enough to do new things.

Every time I visited the family in Connecticut, Mom, Dad, and I ate dinner together. Todd and Tracy were usually busy with their children, leaving my parents and me alone for long evenings. I enjoyed those nights immensely. Since my visits were once a year, I stockpiled big questions to ask about my childhood or theirs. One year, I diagrammed our entire family tree with them over dinner. Another, I asked them about the neighborhoods in Brooklyn where they grew up. My distance made the depth of these conversations natural in that I was a spe-

cial guest, and my probing questions were less intimi-
dating coming from their distant child. In those years, I
settled into a comfort with my parents, and as a trio
we'd have easy evenings, bonding in a way that hadn't
happened in my youth.

But on the night my mother confided in me in her
car, things were different. That night, we drove to a fan-
cy restaurant, and sitting across the table from my father
unnerved me. When I looked into my father's green
eyes, eyes much like mine, I had the same questions my
mother did. What had he done? What did he know?
There he was, an arm's length away, pretending there
was nothing going on at all. Should I force the issue and
bring it up? I thought. I wasn't sure. I buried my discomfort in Gin and Tonics, but it only helped so much.
There was a lie in all this, a lie I was now stuck inside.
Or then again, maybe it was just in my mother's head, a
misunderstanding that we'd laugh about when the air
had been cleared.

I decided the choice here was my mother's, not mine.
She had confided in me, I had accepted it, and that
meant I had to follow her lead. I also realized, while in
my thoughts, that I had no idea where I was and no way
to get home. If I spoke up and caused a scene, I'd be
stuck in the middle of Connecticut, a prospect I found
oddly terrifying. I could have called my brother or a cab
or done a dozen different things, but I didn't think of
them then. Perhaps being with my parents made me feel

more like a child than I realized. I said nothing more to my mother about what she'd told me, and she said nothing to me. The dinner and my visit continued uneventfully.

The next day, I packed my rental car and drove to the airport, grateful the situation hadn't exploded open while I was visiting. With each mile that passed between my family and me, I felt increasing relief to be closer to home. After a few hours, I was almost to the airport, and that's when she called, and left me a message since I was driving. I returned the rental car, went through security, and found the quietest place between two gates to call her back.

She picked up quickly, and I knew the worst was true. She was crying as she told me: he was having an affair. She had confronted him after I left, and at first he had said nothing, but she had pushed and pushed and finally got him to admit that that's why he went to Australia. Her fury and sadness was overwhelming, with overlapping waves of outrage, sadness, questions, and facts. I didn't want to have that conversation on the phone, but it was all we had. Standing near the Hudson News store, in the quietest corner near the airline gates I could find, I couldn't believe this was happening.

As I listened to my mother cry, I couldn't help but watch a businessman eat far too many Dunkin Donuts. I saw a young girl with blond pigtails, sitting on the floor, fight with her brother over an iPad. A few meters away, an older couple debated what to order from McDonald's, their pale hands pointing up at the combo meal deals on the menu. Airports are caverns of trivia, and you're forced to be near people unhappily involved in the most ordinary decisions. In my travels, I've seen, a handful of times, someone crying alone in the empty seats of an unused gate, or yelling at a distant spouse as part of some unresolved relationship drama, but I'd never before been in it myself. Now it was my turn.

I told my mother how sorry I was that this was happening. When she calmed down, I reminded her of my advice to build a support team. She needed to call them now. I told her I was on this team and would do what she needed.

I asked, "Do you want me to get another car and come back to you?"

She said, "No. I need to take care of this on my own. You've been really helpful already, Scott."

I considered driving back anyway, but I wasn't sure there was anything I could do. She soon made a joke about how completely mad this was, laughing about the absurdity of how he was still in the house with her. My sense of humor was her sense of humor, and her laugh made me laugh. She told me she'd figure herself out, and I believed her. I told her to call Todd, but she said she didn't want to yet, a sentiment I ignored; as soon as we hung up, I called him.

I decided, inside of a single moment, that I'd rather her be angry with me for bringing him into this than any other alternative. It was the only way I could make sure she wasn't going to be alone that night; someone else close needed to know. I called him, but there was no answer. I couldn't imagine leaving this news in a message, so I called again and again. I must have called a dozen times, waiting until the last moment to board my plane. Finally, I got through. I told him the thing he didn't want to hear, the thing he and I had both hoped since we were kids that we'd never hear again.

"Todd, I have something important to tell you. Okay?" I said.

Despite 500,000 years of spoken language, there is still no good way for people who love each other to start a hard conversation. Yet we're supposed to give a warning, as if that helps anything at all.

And he replied, as anyone does when they hear close family say this, "Okay."

I continued, "Mom just told me Dad had another affair when he was in Australia. She's really upset, and I need you to call her."

It took a few moments to sink in. The first time we hear something serious, we assume we've heard it wrong. It's only on the third try that our brains catch up with our senses, and the realization that the world has changed begins. He knew I had to hang up soon to catch a plane, but we both knew, in the odd pauses these conversations always have, that something had shifted. The center of our family had moved away from our parents and toward us. I asked him to call her to close the loop of news and let her share the situation with him herself. I didn't like manipulating the situation this way, but I did it anyway. My mother had always been closer to Todd than to me, despite her choice to tell me first, and the sooner I got myself out of the middle, the better. Todd called me back shortly after and told me he'd talked to her and that the three of us were again on the same page. I clicked my seat belt in place, getting ready for the flight and feeling relieved. But I couldn't help but think of my father and mother in that same house together, with hard times looming over them.

I've come to think differently about monsters as an adult than I did as a child. When Terry Gilliam cast the very likeable Michael Palin to play the villain in his film *Brazil*, he offered an unusual theory about evil. He suggested that evil that looks like evil couldn't be as evil as evil that looks like your friend. We can see the bad guy in most films from miles away. Real evil doesn't come at us with a scar over its eye or with a hook for an arm. We don't hear a sinister orchestra play when it walks into the room. In real life, we are on our own to sort out what is evil and what is good and to decide if those terms are cleanly divisible from each other.

Part of being an adult is deciding for ourselves what good and evil are, including the good and evil in our families and in ourselves. Movies and stories betray us in this respect. Angels and demons are harder to recognize in life than in fiction. A person can be an angel to their neighbor but a demon to their coworker, or a saint to a stranger but vicious to their lover. We contain multitudes. We demonize the diagnosis of split personality disorder, but each of us are amalgams of many people, and on each day and in each relationship, we're a slightly different version of ourselves. We only have true consistency in our memories of convenience. We can't be self-aware without admitting those edges and knowing there are many perspectives on who we are. We can be a good person and a bad person simultaneously, but people will only see us as one depending on their point of view.

Who was my father good to? Who in his life got his best? I really don't know. It was certainly no one I knew. And there were so few people in his life. Todd and I often entertained the notion that there was a secret Howard, a part of him only our mother got to see. She'd spent her life telling us about this other side of him, a man who was privately loving, compassionate, and empathetic – someone who thought about me and was interested in what I was doing but just didn't know how to express it directly. This was the Howard she loved to be the spokesperson for. But with this new crisis, we both wondered if she'd been making up this version of him all along. Maybe my father was never present but was something of a ghost, and my relationship with him was more with his absence than his presence.

After I arrived home, the next days were hard, harder for my mother than for me or Todd, but hard nonetheless. Many old memories of hard times came back to me and kept me up at night. I cried in my wife Jill's arms, overwhelmed by how much of what I'd tried to put behind me was present again. She knew about the epic trip to Yellowstone I took with my father as an adult and how hard I'd worked to recover from the failures of that experience. She comforted me and asked why I was so sad, and I was surprised to realize I knew exactly what it was. I was disappointed in myself that I let him hurt me again. I'd never imagined there was anything left he could do that would wound me, and I blamed myself for it. All the work I'd done on myself wasn't enough.

Over the course of those first days, Mom told me what she knew. In the fall of 2011, Howard met a woman online. It was a sad time for him, and he felt alone, joining online chat rooms and social websites to meet people. My sister Tracy had been living next door to my parents for years, and she had moved away months prior, taking her four children, his grandchildren, with her. Perhaps this loss wounded him in ways he didn't know how to handle, but he never spoke of it. He didn't reach out to Todd or me or invest more in his relationship with Todd's children, who still lived just minutes away. Instead, he went online to seek comfort from strangers.

Soon he met a woman named Crissy on a website called Fubar.com (a prescient name, all things considered). It's a service that bills itself as the Web's first online bar, where users can buy virtual drinks for friends using *fu-bucks*. It was embarrassing to explore it myself, but I did and discovered it was much like a bar, with a mix of people looking to socialize and those looking for romantic encounters. Regardless of my father's intentions, he and Crissy soon exchanged emails with each other, and their connection grew stronger.

She knew my father was married, and he knew she was going through a divorce. Somewhere during the fall of 2011, he proposed the idea of flying to visit her in Australia. She initially refused. When he explained the nature of his "cockeyed marriage," she agreed. In my father's eyes, his marriage to my mother had always had fundamental problems, hinged on the fact that they'd married too young. At nineteen, his father threatened to throw him out of the house, and his engagement to my mother bought him time. Soon after, my oldest brother Todd was born. And two years later, Tracy came into this world. Four years later, it was my turn, and by the time I was eight years old, my father wanted to escape from his marriage and had his first affair.

But if the marriage had fundamental problems, why hadn't he tried to repair the marriage or end it in the three decades since the first affair? I asked him this question, but he had no answer. He held an amazing capacity for duality in his mind, seeing himself both as a powerless victim of forces beyond anyone's control and a heroic figure. Depending on the question I asked, he'd pick one or the other or ramble his way between both. His marriage to my mother was a mystery to him too perhaps. If it was so bad, why didn't he leave? If it was so good, why risk it on affairs? It didn't make sense to me, and I don't think it did to him either.

Howard's lies piled up. They were his favorite kind: the half lies. His fear of turning seventy might have been real, but that wasn't the primary reason for the trip or its destination. Whatever feelings of sadness or despair he felt, he kept them to himself and worked out this new plan of escape all on his own, with no thoughts for how the rest of us would feel once we knew the facts, which was inevitable.

I didn't know what to say when Mom shared the details. It was shocking and demoralizing. I felt like how I imagine the children of criminals feel. I had to tell Jill about the details to help me absorb the fact that this was happening. It was only listening to the words come out of my mouth that made it real and not merely something in my mind. I felt embarrassed to have encouraged him to go to Australia. I felt ashamed to be his son, both for what he was putting my mother through and what it might mean for me and my sense of family. I felt hate for him, the old hate, the hate I'd worked hard through my life to leave behind: the hate of a child in a family divided by its father, and the hate fueled by a separated family thrown back together without healing the wounds that had divided us. I didn't sleep well anymore. It was as if someone had swept my legs out from under me, and when I turned to look at who did it, I saw my father nearby, walking away without even looking me in the eyes.

I ran through the possibilities of what might happen next. Where was this situation going to go? One possibility was that my father had had a fling, a chance happening, a tryst. That he'd recognize his mistake and apologize, asking for forgiveness. His entire adult life had been dependent on my mother, and she was and had always been his best friend. But the months of premeditation in his trip and the weeks of silence when he returned made this less likely. He'd also already purchased tickets to return to Australia. Before I'd arrived for my visit, he had already planned to return but told none of us. This had been a slow, careful, thoughtful choice, and none of it had involved thinking of my mother. If none of his choices considered my mother's feelings, there was no chance he considered mine.

For the first time in my life, I considered changing my name. This surprised even me, as I had always liked the sound of the name of my family. For every basketball team I've ever played for, I was simply called Berkun, and even today, many friends call me by that name. I know my family history for four generations, and I'm proud of where I'm from. I've always felt my achievements honored my parents and everyone else who shares my name. But after I learned of what my father had done, every time I signed a contract or read my mail, I'd see my father's name in my own, and it bothered me. I wanted no reminder that my life was tied to his, as the very idea of family and his role, or lack thereof, in it had been revealed as foreign to me.

I didn't feel betrayed by his affair. At least that wasn't the primary feeling I had. I wasn't angry that my parents' marriage might end, as sad as it might have been. My father could have divorced my mother or moved to Australia or done a thousand other things I'd have preferred he didn't, and I wouldn't have taken it personally, as it had nothing to do directly with me in my adult life. Instead, my anger came from his silence. There was no attempt to explain himself, and I felt I deserved an explanation. He'd kept a secret of his own making, a secret that, now revealed, left all of us – my mother, my brother, and me – to sort everything out for ourselves. Had he called me to tell me the news himself, I could have at least respected him for being accountable for his decisions and tending to their potential impact on me, but that call never came. Instead, I saw him as a coward, a person afraid to take responsibility for the consequences of his choices.

Days passed as I realized I wasn't going to hear from him. I decided I would write to him myself. I refined and refined this note until it was simple and pragmatic, divorced from my feelings about anything. Taking the highest ground and giving all the benefits of doubt I could muster, I sent this:

From: Scott Berkun
Date: Sunday, June 24, 2012 9:25 AM
To: Howard Berkun
Subject: Your legacy with the Berkun family

Mom told me you are leaving. She told me you know that I know. Yet you haven't called or written to tell me yourself what you're doing.

There may be more to your story but you have not made any effort to share it: I can only assume her version is true. With this I'm devastated by the choices you've made. I can't express how hurt, upset and disappointed I am. But that's not why I'm writing.

You need sound advice. I do not believe you have close friends or family who can give you good council. Even if you do, I doubt you've made use of them to inform your feelings and decisions these last months.

I suspect you have been isolating yourself from those closest to you for some time, denying yourself the benefit of the honest perspective only those who care most about you will give. You told me you think I'm the ace in the deck, yet I can't remember the last time you asked me for advice.

My advice is this: As the patriarch you will leave a legacy that will carry on for generations. This last chapter will define how Todd and I remember you, and how your grandchildren and their children understand who you were. How did you treat us? How did you treat Mom? How did you handle good times and tough times? Tara, Aaron, Josh, Jessica, Aidan, Gavin, me, Tracy and Todd will all carry on and you have invested much of your life in providing for us.

Yet your recent choices abandon us. You're rejecting your family in favor of a person you only recently met. You're trading 50 years with Mom, 46 years with Todd and 40 with me, entire lifetimes, for something you barely know. We can only feel we never meant much if you are willing to vanish to the other side of the world, and trade us in for so little.

You've made choices without explanation and little forethought into the consequences for us. If you needed more from me or Todd or Mom, or had issues to solve, or painful feelings you were dealing with, you never gave us a chance to help you.

Every day is new. You can still try to seek advice. But now you are confused and lost and alone which is a bad place to be when making choices that define the rest of your life. If you continue on this path your legacy will be rejecting your children *and your best-friend of 50 years, repeating for us the most painful episode of our lives when you left nearly 30 years ago. Your story will be defined primarily by abandonment and selfishness.*

What legacy do you want to leave with the family you spent your life building? Please keep that in mind as you make your next decisions.

Love -Scott

When I wrote this letter, I didn't know I'd be writing a memoir about my family. As a writer, I never imagined that if I wrote a memoir, my father, of all people, would be at its center. As I read this email now, I can't help but notice the word "legacy." Of the many reasons I'm writing this book, one is so my nieces and nephews have one telling of this story they can read if, even decades from now, they become curious. Most families rely on memory, and the story changes with each telling of the tale. I don't want more ghosts haunting my family. To put into words what I know and feel is an act of hope for the future, a faith that whoever reads it can put it to use. I didn't know it then, but my questioning my father's legacy in that email led me to question my own. But I went to bed that night without a reply, wondering what would happen next and if the high road was the right one.

The first fable I learned about fathers was from *Star Wars*. The discovery of the true identity of Darth Vader shocked me in a way no movie or book had before. The American Film Institute lists Vader, in his *The Empire Strikes Back* appearance, as the third best villain of all time, ranked only behind Hannibal Lecter from *The Silence of the Lambs* and Norman Bates from *Psycho*. I've noticed many of the films made by Lucas and Spielberg have plots defined by distant and absent fathers (*Raiders of the Lost Ark: The Last Crusade, E.T., Hook, Close Encounters of the Third Kind, War of the Worlds*), and it's a theme that runs through Shakespeare's *Hamlet* and even Shelley's *Frankenstein*. There is a long history in almost every culture, in literature and mythology, of stories of fathers who weren't very good as parents.

But as a boy, the only story I knew was Vader's, and I'd grow up making my own comparisons between me and Luke Skywalker, and my father and Vader. It's a disturbing memory now, but I remember sitting on my father's shoulders when he took me to a *Star Wars* publicity event to see the one and only Darth Vader. Of course, it wasn't really Darth Vader but instead some out-of-work actor in a rented Darth Vader suit, but these trivialities are irrelevant to a young boy. I was going to see someone from the greatest film of all time as far as I was concerned.

I only remember this story because of an old photo I've seen dozens of times, a photo now lost to history. In the photo, I was six or seven years old, still small and light enough that my father didn't mind carrying me around. It was at a Toys 'R' Us store, and we were waiting in a crowded line, packed with screaming kids and parents at the end of their ropes of patience. My mom was there too, as it must have been she who took the photo. It's strange to me now how we are fans of evil, that we'd sell merchandise and hold events to celebrate a person, real or fictitious, who epitomizes what we're hoping, in our real lives, to avoid. Perhaps part of the power of stories is they allow us to relate to evil in a way far safer than examining the bad, however silent and repressed, inside ourselves.

I can't think of this day visiting Vader with my father without recalling what it was like to see *Star Wars* for the second time. I don't remember what it was like the first time, because I was too young and without expectations. I didn't know what it was like to love a film that much. But the second time I saw the film, I'd been anticipating it for days. I remember sitting in the front row of the balcony at the huge single auditorium theater in Bay Terrace, looking down as wave after wave of families walked down the aisles, filling in the seats below me. I nervously ate from the bag of popcorn in my hand, hoping with each and every second that the film would start.

It was in the second film that the world of *Star Wars* shifted from magic to despair. I remember the drive home after seeing *The Empire Strikes Back* and feeling deeply disturbed. I'd never seen a film that hit me so hard emotionally, generating feelings I didn't even know that I had. I was sad, I was angry, and I was confused all at the same time, and thinking about these feelings didn't make them go away – it made them stronger. When Vader told Luke that he is his father, the defining moment of the film, I thought it had to be a trick. It was incomprehensible that a hero so good could have come from someone so bad. I wishfully decided there had to be some other explanation. It was magical thinking, believing that something couldn't be true simply because of how much I didn't want it to be.

Luke's horror was twofold, and it was the combination that was more than my young brain could handle. Knowing little of his father's life meant Luke's father was a mystery to him, a neutral figure. Maybe he was a good man, maybe he was a bad man. The shock that he was alive would have been difficult enough to handle. To learn at the same time that his father was an enthusiastically bad man, a figure that stood against all that Luke had just learned to love, was devastating. And the last touch was that this discovery was made only moments after Vader had nearly killed Luke, his only son. Why would Vader choose this time, and this moment, to reveal himself? Why not send a nice box of Stormtrooper chocolates or a gift-wrapped light saber with "To Luke, From Dad" monogrammed on the handle? The answer is that Vader was someone who confused control with love. Vader believed the only way to get what he wanted was to force it to happen, pun intended, and what he wanted was all that mattered.

Few people know that the evil of Vader was likely a reflection of Lucas' own experience. George's father rejected his interest in filmmaking when George was just a boy. His father wanted George to join the family business, much like Vader wanted "to rule the galaxy together." Whatever the motivations were for Lucas, and the screenwriters Leigh Brackett and Lawrence Kasdan, I know I'd never seen a movie that disturbed me so deeply before. It twisted the fabric of good and bad in a way that has stayed on my mind all of my life.

When we left the theater after seeing *The Empire Strikes Back*, I asked my mother if it was true: was Vader really Luke's father, or was he lying? She smiled at me in that way that said there's a truth she knew I didn't want to hear. I pressed on, and she told me that yes, it was true, but I still didn't believe it. It was only when I saw the next film, *Return of the Jedi*, that I accepted the truth. The redemption of Vader in *Return of the Jedi*, where he sacrifices himself to save his son, came to mind often as a private fantasy. I wondered what I could do that would impress my father enough to change him, or in the parlance of the film, reveal the good that had been in him all along. I wondered how I could achieve something worthy of his goodness, worthy of his love. If only I were better at basketball or school or something, I thought.

Lucas made three more films about Vader, an attempt to redeem this father figure even further than the first trilogy did. It's no surprise that Lucas and his father reconciled during those many intervening years. Vader now easily fits into a long series of misunderstood monsters, going back through Frankenstein, the Greek Myths, and even Aesop's Fables. The pattern of the misunderstood monster is a creature who suffers a deep wound early in its life, a wound it never recovers from. As the creature's personality grows around that injury, covering it up and patching it over, the foundation of the creature's identity that forms is incomplete. With each year that passes, it puts more and more layers of experience above that wound, so much that it can't see the wound anymore. And the deeply buried pain hurts so much that the creature struggles to be good to others. The depth keeps the wound safe from further injury but also prevents it from ever healing. Dr. Frankenstein hurt the creature he made by instantly abandoning him after he was born. The creature wanted the love of his father but received only hate and rejection. His father's response to his very birth turned the child into a wounded creature of rage, a monster that would take his father's name, forever seeking revenge from the person who'd given him life but not love.

I don't want to see my father as a monster. We all suffer old wounds we don't have the courage to heal, as healing is one of the most painful things we can do. Healing requires being vulnerable, often to the very people who have wounded us. There are many good things my father did for our family and for me. He worked hard to provide for us and kept us safe. But because he couldn't see his own wounds and how they'd changed him, he never realized the biggest danger to the family wasn't outside the house but was inside him instead.

Irving Berkun, my father's father, was the quietest man I'd ever met. When I was a child, we visited my grandparents' house in Elmont on Sundays. He'd sit quietly on his puffy orange couch, a couch covered with those ridiculous plastic covers. Those strange covers, popular in those days, signified a postponement of living, of choosing to preserve the couch instead of enjoying the pleasure of sitting on it. My grandparents' miserable little black dog Poochie spent his hours hiding under that couch, growling at anyone who dared to reach underneath. They never clipped his nails, so they twisted in knots at the edge of his paws. Poochie was the first dog I met that I didn't like. He was an insane guard dog, driven mad by neglect, or perhaps abuse, protecting himself from everyone instead of protecting his family from danger.

Irving, my grandfather, was always watching professional wrestling when we visited. He'd stare into that television as if he and it were the only things left on the planet. His social skills, even with his own grandchildren, were nonexistent. I didn't receive a single smile or pat on the head from him in my life. In my entire life, I don't remember him ever saying a word to me. As sad as that sounds, I can only imagine the tragedy of being born his son. What must he have been like then? Irving had served in WWII in the Merchant Marine, perhaps in a line of work that required little talking. Even after the war, he was often away at sea, preferring the silence of the ocean to being in his own home.

My father's mother, Tessie, was always kind to me. She had warmth and a sharp humor that made those visits fun. Every time I walked in that door, she'd smile and hug me, offering hot Jell-O, which sounds disgusting now but was sweet and warm then, and I'd accept her offer of it more often than not. I'd sit at the small folding table in her kitchen, drinking the hot Jell-O and eating Entenmann's coffeecake. We never stayed there more than a few hours, a short enough slice of my life that the visits were never more than a curiosity, a visit to a world I knew I never had to live in.

As the oldest son, my father had been the center of his mother's world when he was young. She had convinced him he was brilliant and great at everything. The price for this attention was her demand of perfection in everything he did. A grade of ninety-five on a spelling test was not good enough, and she pushed him hard, more through guilt and shame than encouragement. When he turned fifteen years old, Tessie's mother became mentally ill, demanding long hours of care from her every day. With Irving also away so often, Howard was on his own. He'd recently skipped a grade level, a choice made with Tessie's encouragement, which made the social challenges of school hard for him. He struggled with school and with making friends. All his life he'd been groomed to believe how special he was, but now the world around him told him something else. Even his mother, the one person who loved him the most, abandoned him and left him alone. It was a painful time for him, the worst time of his young life.

There were only two possible ways for young Howard to resolve this situation. One was to realize he wasn't the amazing person his mother had told him he was all his life. The other was to decide there was something wrong with the world. He decided the latter. It may be too much to say it's something he consciously decided. Or perhaps he was already too far gone in his own narcissism to consider alternatives at all. Instead of being humbled by his situation, his arrogance grew. Instead of learning to connect with people, he stayed away. Four years later, he met meet my mother. She protected him from the world and enabled his immaturity, in many of the same ways Tessie had. A decade later, I was born, and when I was eight years old, he moved away.

The story my father has told me more than any other about his childhood is about a time he was playing baseball in a park in Brooklyn. His mother watched him play, standing on the sidelines near first base. He was up at bat and hit a ground ball into the infield. He ran as fast as he could to first base, and just before the throw came in from the shortstop, he stepped loudly on the bag. But the first baseman and the umpire both thought he was out. An argument started, and the umpire asked Tessie what she saw. Howard looked to her, hoping she'd come to the defense of her oldest and most amazing son. I imagine the look on her face, slowly looking at him, then back to the base, and then at him again. Finally, she said, "He was out." My father was devastated. He'd wanted her support, but she gave it away to strangers. My father believes she knew he was safe but didn't want to argue on his behalf, preferring to please other people instead. I can imagine young Howard brooding all the way home and for days to come, feeling betrayed. The only person he'd trusted in his life had abandoned him, and he'd never give that trust to anyone again.

My father was seventy years old the last time I heard this story. The event itself took place sixty years ago. There is no one else alive who shares this memory, as my grandmother passed away in 2005. I know he never brought the memory to her to see how his recollections compared with hers. Given what we know about memory, it's impossible to know what really happened. Maybe she wasn't paying attention and responded with a shrug, which disappointed Howard. Or perhaps he was out, and the first baseman was right. Should she have defended him anyway and lied about it? But maybe the facts aren't important in memories like these. Every time my father tells this story, there's a meaning that's important to him in the present that has little to do with the past.

Year after year, emotions filter our memories, shifting their focus. The details we fixate on express feelings we've yet to resolve or understand. Each time I've heard this story, its point is his feeling of abandonment, a notion that echoes my own feelings about my father. He has played the same role in many of the childhood memories I have. He wasn't there. He wasn't an ally. He chose the world over me more often than not. We both share the same kind of wound. Where I hope we differ is in what we've done about it. He never gave up his grip on blaming his mother, which left him with only one hand for experiencing the emotions of life.

Leo Buscaglia, the author of the powerful book *Living, Loving, Learning*, defined an adult as someone capable of making choices. We are not slaves to the past, saying lines from a script written long ago, a script given to us by our parents. A mature adult instead is aware of their own patterns and the experiences that created them, and can, with effort, choose to go another way. But it requires work to reach maturity, work few people do. Abraham Maslow, of the eponymous hierarchy, called this process of a person living to their potential "self-actualization." When we're stuck in the past, protecting old wounds or fighting with ghosts in our minds, we are fractions of who we could be.

Assuming Buscaglia and Maslow are right and that it's possible to leave the past behind, who is willing to do this kind of work? Maybe one person in five? It's far easier to go with the grain of the lives we find ourselves in, even if we're unfulfilled. Few people willingly choose to take on the challenge, and of those who do, it's often a crisis that motivates the attempt: a failing marriage, a near-death experience, or a deep depression. It's only when things are the worst that we have enough desperation to change. I sent my email to my father with hope that this was that time for him, that finally after all this time, he'd faced something too big to explain away, forcing open paths he'd denied before.

The situation had its effect on me too. I discovered long ago that writing in my journal, meditating, and exercising are three habits I must keep to stay aware of myself. If I'm an easygoing person, it's because of those habits. But in those first weeks of this new world, I struggled to concentrate. I had nightmares. My mind wandered easily to the past, stuck in old, sad memories like the ones I've shared in this book. It felt like a curse, as no matter how much I worked through my feelings in the present, it created waves of old emotions back from the past. I took comfort in talking to Jill, Todd, and close friends. Jill and I were seeing a marriage counselor at the time, and my feelings surfaced there too. No matter what I did, those feelings and memories stayed at the front of my mind.

One gift of art is catharsis. Art can express feelings we struggle with, helping us to follow along. There are three films I watch when I'm having the hardest of times: *The Thin Red Line*, *Fight Club*, and *Magnolia*. Jill knows I'm in a bad way when she comes home to find me on the couch watching one of them. Watching dark films during dark times is a curious therapy, but it works for me. The darker the story, the more contrast I find with my struggles. Dark stories remind me how much worse the human experience can be than whatever I'm currently struggling with. And when the film ends, and I return to my own world, I discover my feelings have moved, even if only slightly, toward a better place. In hard times, small wins change lives.

I've seen *Magnolia* many times, but this time I found myself most absorbed by a scene I'd never thought much about. There is a moment in the film where young Stanley Spector, having just had the worst moment of his life, embarrassing himself on national television, discovers something important. The action slows down, and the camera moves in close. In a moment of existential recognition about the strangeness of life, he says to himself, "This is something that happens." When he utters these words, a calm overtakes him, and the judgment of the world fades away. And something in this moment, Stanley's acceptance of the absurdity of life, touched me where I needed to be touched, and I cried. I was like Stanley as a boy during my parents' first separation: sad and lost in an ocean of distant adults. Something released in me that I didn't realize I'd been holding on to so tightly for so long. My father's new affair put my emotions back in time to those dark days, and there were things back there that wanted to come out. I wrote the phrase down in my journal and on the whiteboard near my writing desk: *This is something that happens.*

This phrase, as my mantra, kept me from falling into denial. It prevented me from indulging in indifference. It stopped me when I thought for too many hours about what I could have or should have done in the past. It was a reminder that the unraveling of my family was real, and I had to accept it even if I'd never understand it. Far worse things happen to far better families. I was lucky to be so old and so far away when this happened to my family a second time.

At midnight a few days later, my father replied to my email. It was the longest and most personal letter he'd ever written to me. I shared it with Todd, who had never seen anything like it either.

From: Howard Berkun
Date: Mon, 25 Jun 2012 23:47:28 -0400
To: Scott Berkun
Subject: RE: Your legacy with the Berkun family

hi scott,

Yes, i have not acted well. Not speaking to you on this very important matter. Its not an easy topic to discuss, let alone with the ones who love mom so deeply.

i have not succeeded in my life for various reasons. the biggest being living life to someone elses wishes. Doing the right thing as my mom would wish. Living with previously made decisions and although unhappy, finding it harder or impossible to change course. Sort of doing the expected thing would be most popular to many, but not right for yourself. e.g. you changing careers, discarding microsoft for a new path.

i attempted a breakout 35 yrs ago, finally doing something selfish and pleasureable and rewarding. Guilt, stopped me from carrying through.

[...]

Generally speaking, regarding death as you alluded to, the way i see it, i have been sitting and working here endlessly and being unhappy and waiting to die.

And so, i went and chatted with another, and started awakening. And after a while life started to overwhelm the rest. And I dont know where i go. Where life takes me. But there is more to life than building a legacy.. Life should be for the living. And as for building throughout my life, it hasnt resulted in gratification. All i have to show here is walls, windows, and trees.

Dont want to hurt anyone. But, i hurt. I hurt for a long time. and it never gets better.

I love you very much
Dad
keep up the communication

A lifetime of my father's silences ended with this letter. It was hard to take in, and I found myself going back to read it many times. He'd never once mentioned feeling like a failure in anything in his life, at least not to me. He was proud of providing for his family, proud of the small company he had started, and proud of some things he shouldn't have been proud of. Had all that been a grand lie, and this was the truth? Or was this a way to justify his recent actions? Or some of both? There was no way to know. It came all at once like an old forgotten dam breaking open, burying everything that had been assumed to be safe in the wake of powerful, old waters.

From one perspective, the letter made complete sense. My father excelled at harboring feelings, something he'd learned from his own parents. He'd held each of his children, and my mother, in silent contempt, blaming us in the privacy of his own mind. Like many men of his generation, expressing feelings was foreign, almost absurd to him, and that in itself hid a multitude of problems. He'd only bring his feelings to light, often with coaching from my mother, when he needed to justify an offense. He'd pull from his inventory of ancient grievances as justification: "If I hurt you, I'm sorry, but you hurt me on December 2, 1984 at 11:05 a.m." His life-long misery described in the email, if true, was another secret he'd kept in his back pocket. Perhaps he was Thoreau's average man, living in quiet desperation and sharing the truth only now when it was harder than ever to want to help him. Or perhaps that was the best story he could imagine for explaining himself.

The middle of the email, which I've omitted, was a painful ramble of accusations against Todd, Tracy, my mother, and me, spanning many years. He mentioned how I sent flowers on Mother's Day, but not Father's Day, a deliberate choice I had made after our failed trip together to Yellowstone. He listed his disappointment at gifts to Todd and Tracy that didn't work out the way he'd wanted. It was a jumble of intense, unsorted feelings, making it hard to know what he was hoping to express. The question I was left with was: now what? He'd responded. What should I do, if anything?

Jill taught me long ago that the place to start in emotional situations is with acceptance. It doesn't matter how small the thing is that we accept, but when someone makes themselves vulnerable, we have to ask if we want to continue the conversation. If we do, we must start on their terms, even if just by saying, "I understand how you feel, as I've felt that way myself." This meant I had to think through what he'd said carefully, looking for something to agree with, something I could honestly acknowledge. Anything else I wanted to say would have to wait.

I knew all this might be a manipulation, that his email was more about him rationalizing his choices, but if that were true, I'd know soon enough. For the sake of my mother, my brother, and what was left of my family, there was advice he needed that he wouldn't hear from anyone else. I decided that I alone could give him this advice, and that was the best thing I could do for him, my family, and myself.

From: Scott Berkun
Date: Tuesday, June 26, 2012 5:56 PM
To: Howard
Subject: Re: Your legacy with the Berkun family

Thanks for sharing how you really feel. I understand. I'm sorry you feel so much pain.

I have many thoughts on what you have written, but you haven't asked for my opinion so I won't offer any unless that's what you want. I'd like for you to be happy and to help you. How can I help?

As a son to both of you there is only so much I can do. I hope you'll forgive me for giving you two unsolicited pieces of advice:

1) If you want to move on, hire a mediator. You need a third party to help you do what's best for each of you. Given the baggage you mention and the intense stress both of you are under right now, neither of you is doing your best thinking. Give yourself the benefit of a calm, neutral expert who has significant experience with the situation you are in. It will cost little and if you learn one thing it will have been worthwhile given what's at stake.

2) If you expect to continue a relationship with Mom, of any kind, see a marriage counselor together. They are experts in the crisis you are in. They can provide tools and perspective to help you both, and provide a needed neutral perspective on everything (I say this as a man who has been seeing a marriage counselor for over a year). If you go and don't like it, you've lost nothing. If you decide to move on, a visit to a counselor will help you both relate to each other in the future, which is likely given the children, family and everything else you currently share.

Love, -Scott

While this email conversation continued, I talked to Mom daily on the phone and gave similar advice. I wanted to avoid playing a mediator role in any way. I'd done this as a teenager for some of their fights and didn't want to do it again.

My father replied two days later. He took my advice better than I expected, yet worse too – more complications. He agreed with my suggestions but wanted to wait until he returned from Australia in a few weeks to do anything about them. He made no mention of his behavior or how I might feel about it. He seemed almost excited, which was hard to understand:

Thanks for the email, and your consideration and understanding. It means a lot to me that you understand. Anything else..?? Ears are open !!

The ears were the easy part, I thought; it was his heart he had trouble with. Somewhere between his ears and his heart, the wiring didn't work right, and that's how we'd ended up here in the first place. But I knew this was as close as he was ever going to get to asking how I felt, so I wrote a short and honest reply.

From: Scott Berkun
Date: Monday, July 2, 2012 at 9:36 AM
To: Howard
Subject: Re: Your legacy with the Berkun family

> Anything else..?? Ears are open !!

About you: What advice would you have for me if I told you I met a woman in France on a business trip and was separating from Jill to be with her? I think you'd tell me that there was a luster and romance to the new, and as the relationship becomes less a fantasy and more a reality, many of the problems I was trying to flee would surface. Traveling 15,000 miles to be with someone is a powerful tale of romance, but that power fades. I caution you to keep that in mind as your family hangs in the balance.

About me: I have many thoughts and feelings about what has happened. I'm hurt by your choices as I am still part of the family unit you have cast aside. It's likely I will never be able to 'come home' again as there won't be a home to go to. I'm also angry about the way you handled your choices. We were together as a family last week and you could have chosen to talk to me, or the family together, about what you have done and are deciding to do. You could have at least made certain I heard about your choices from you, rather than through Mom. As a result this drama played out in a very stressful way for me, and

68

*put Todd and I in crisis mode trying to figure out what was
going on and figure out what we should do. I was deeply
wounded once by you leaving when I was young, and you have
wounded me again in similar fashion as an adult.*

I wish you the best. Love,

-Scott

I sent that email on July 2. To this day, he's never replied. A few days later, he got on a plane to return to
Australia. Without a thought, he left his wounded family
behind him to fall backward into the limbo of the past.

TWO

....

BROTHER AND SISTER

Until I was eight years old, Todd and I shared a bedroom. We got along well even though he was six years older than me. My childhood friend Craig had a brother the same age as Todd, and he picked on Craig often, using his size to push Craig around. Many older siblings take advantage, but Todd never did. He was friendly and fair despite the countless advantages he had over me in size and smarts. We shared the same creative spirit too, spending long hours inventing worlds of Matchbox cars in the basement, with maze-like tracks for them to ride on. In the hallway upstairs, we'd have paper airplane flying competitions, carefully drawing logos and names like "X-15" or "Apollo 11" on the wings of the loose-leaf paper we used. Then we'd see which of us could throw their planes the farthest from our bedroom, maybe out past the stairs, or if we got lucky, all the way to the couch in the living room.

The bond we shared happened on its own and grew strong but never reached the radar of our parents. It seemed our connection was a mild annoyance to them and Tracy too. Tracy, as the middle child and only daughter, often felt left out. She never found her way inside the connection we had, despite the attempts everyone made to bring her in. We didn't mean to keep her out, but she easily got upset, sensitive to the smallest of unintended slights, wearing away the motivation to bring her closer inside.

During dinner, Todd and I made each other laugh doing Monty Python routines or jokes and skits we'd invented ourselves. My parents were sometimes annoyed by our banter despite its innocence. We weren't making fun of anyone at the table, but they'd ask us to stop sometimes as if we were disrupting everyone. I realize now it was foreign to the family to see two people who genuinely got along. Anyone could have joined in our playfulness, and occasionally they did, but a certain joy was required that wasn't in abundance. My parents never took the golden opportunity of rewarding and encouraging a powerful bond of brotherhood that formed all on its own.

Looking back now, the relationship between me and Todd was the strongest in the family, though no one, including us, thought about it that way. No one told us being close as siblings was rare and worth protecting. Howard and his younger brother, who were also six years apart in age, didn't talk to each other for most of my childhood. The story I was always told was that Danny was a difficult person, a story I've long doubted and have more reasons to doubt today. Even my mother's sibling relationships were complicated at best. Yet Todd and I never heard much praise for what we had and still have. It's the things a family is silent about that say more than what they talk about all the time.

For years, Todd was a counselor at the same summer camp I went to, the Samuel Field Y in Little Neck, Long Island. We'd ride the same bus to and from the campgrounds every day. I was ten years old when this picture was taken, and Todd was sixteen years old, which means our parents were separated at the time. It's clear that even at this young age, I was destined to be a wiseass and a troublemaker.

At night, Todd and I used to listen to radio shows on our old alarm clock, the kind with the black and white flip cards for the minutes and seconds. One evening, the story was a thriller about a group of vampires that was stalking young high school students. It scared me in a way that was thrilling and fun while the story was playing, but that left me terrified when it was over. Todd shut off the radio, and we went to bed. In the silence, we wished each other goodnight, but I knew I was far too scared to sleep.

I asked my brother, in a whisper: "Hey, Todd. What happens if a vampire comes in the night?"

It was a serious question, and he heard the fear in my voice. It was a different thing to listen to these stories at my age than at his.

He thought for a moment and then replied, "Don't worry; I'm bigger, so it will get me first. I have more blood than you do."

This was great news to me, a fantastic insight into vampire tactics. I felt comforted, and my fears faded away. He seemed so certain, which relieved me, and I rolled over and went to sleep. Todd of course stayed up all night, terrified by his own logic. He took an imaginary bullet for me. It was a small thing, a tiny shared moment that has stayed with me forever. Inside that memory is something important about Todd's nature and the effect the little decisions he made in my presence had on me.

Todd was almost a parent, in the emotional sense of the word, in those early years. He didn't possess all of the knowledge adults have, but he shared the most important possession we have, which is time. Since he was wiser, even if not by that much, the time we shared let him nudge me toward confidence in dozens of little ways. I've asked him, as an adult, why he did this. He didn't get much positive encouragement from our parents. And few older siblings were so kind. His answer was that he didn't want me to struggle with the things he had struggled with. He didn't want me to have the same wounds, the same bad experiences that he'd had when he was my age. He did it simply because it was the right thing to do, and he wanted to be the kind of person who did those things. For all the tension I felt in the absence of my father, it was counterbalanced by the purity of my brother's love. It's one of the great good fortunes of my life to have grown up with Todd as my brother.

One year in summer camp, I was afraid to go in the deep pool, a pool deep enough that I couldn't stand and had to swim. I'd done all of the lessons in the kid's pool, but I was afraid of moving on, so scared that I fell behind all my friends. Since Todd was a counselor and had been volunteering that week at the pool, he saw me refusing to go in day after day. Eventually he'd had enough. He walked over to where I was.

I saw him coming and instantly knew his intentions, but he was bigger and stronger. He grabbed me easily despite my flailing attempts to escape. I screamed and kicked, demanding to be put down, but he didn't give up. In one motion, he leaned his shoulders back and to the left to get enough momentum and then threw me right over the stone edge of the pool and into the deep water. I was furious as he threw me, already thinking about how I was going to fight him when I got out. Through my anger, I didn't care how much bigger he was. I remember being in the air, waiting to land, planning to start swimming at the first possible moment. And then I hit the water, muttering to myself as I gritted my teeth. Immediately I swam as fast as I could to get to him. But then, mid-stroke, I had a realization: I was swimming in the deep water! I didn't stop to think about it, as all I wanted was revenge, but as I swam, I couldn't get the fact that I was swimming in the deep pool out of my mind. It was fun in the deep water, I realized. It was just like swimming anywhere except for the thrill of knowing how deep it was below. I was strangely proud of myself for being there in that moment, even though I was still angry with Todd for putting me there.

I told myself I'd explore this new experience for a moment, and then when I was done, I'd go after him. But by the time I left the pool, I'd forgotten I was angry at all. My first breakthrough about fear had happened, and I didn't know it. Without saying a word, my brother had set me on a course to grow up to be a braver man, as this story of the ethereality of fear would come to my mind hundreds of times in my life. I don't know when it's right or wrong to force someone to do something, but I do know if you love someone, sometimes you have to push and hope they'll understand. Being thrown into the deep water changed me. There was no one else in my life who threw me into anything. It was a day that made me a braver man – a man brave enough to write this book.

I've always been confused by my father's confidence and lack thereof, how his great love for baseball hadn't compelled him to try out for his high school team. The missing piece of that puzzle, and of his childhood, might have been he needed someone older, someone he trusted, to encourage him and to convert that notion he had about what he could be into an attempt to achieve it. Whatever the cause of his doubts, he passed them on to me. When I switched from baseball to basketball, whatever limited interest my father had in my athletics faded. And at the same time, basketball had grown into the most important thing in my life. It was the one thing I had the most confidence in, and it shaped the way my friends thought of me. But I'd never played for an organized league. It wasn't like today where most children play in soccer or other sports teams from an early age. I had big dreams of playing in the NBA but was ignorant of even the most basic steps to take to discover what potential I had.

When I was twelve years old, Todd told me to try out for the junior varsity basketball team at the Samuel Field YMHA. I was a year too young, and despite how cocky I was, I didn't think I could do it. I played for hours every day in the city parks near our house, but an organized league was real, with referees, foul shots, and everything.

It was a new world, and I was intimidated and too proud to admit to my fears. I told Todd it was a mistake, and he stopped talking about it. But that little push, that single mention, was enough for me to look at the tryout schedule. They were a few weeks away. Still hoping for a way out, I asked my mother if she could take me, half hoping she'd say no. But she said yes. She usually said yes to helping me do the things I was trying to do. With each little step, it became clear there was no reason left not to try, so I did.

To my surprise, I made the team. It was an enormous triumph to get validation from strangers that I was good at something, but I don't remember a celebration at home. I don't recall a mention from my father. It was, like everything else in life, only worthy of a shrug from him. This began a divide that would become enormous, the gap between the praise I received outside the house and inside. No one inside the house knew or understood what these achievements meant to me or cared to join in celebrating them. It would fuel my fire to want to leave home, as I didn't feel home was a place where people were invested in how I felt about my dreams, however ridiculous they were to the rest of the world. Of course, I'd never play in the NBA – I was barely good enough to play for a small college – but that's never the point with dreams. At the time, it was the dream I was investing in, and anyone who wasn't helping me make those investments put themselves on the outside of my young life.

I played at the Y for another year before making my high school basketball team as a junior, another triumph. I was so proud that day, the first Berkun to ever play a varsity sport, but no one else cared. I was a starter on the team as a senior and eventually played a year for Drew University. Throughout those years, basketball was my life; it was my primary source of identity and self-worth. I wasn't tall or particularly gifted. It was through discipline, study, and smarts that I was able to achieve what I did. It was how I learned that passion changed little in my life if I didn't convert it into work.

I discovered I could do some of the things I saw Larry Bird or Michael Jordan do simply by slowing down what I saw. I'd study their moves, breaking them into small steps I could practice individually. And then by putting the pieces together and doing them slowly over and over until they became familiar, eventually it would become natural to do it faster and faster again. Soon I'd be able to do something in a game I couldn't do before. Leading a project or writing a book demands the same attitude of divide and conquer and dedication to practice. There isn't a single professional achievement in life that I don't link back to what I learned from basketball. I don't know who I'd be without it. And it all started from Todd's little pushes and nudges. There was no one else looking out for me in that way.

The absence of my father's interest in what I was doing was the defining element of my childhood; it made me strong, and it made me weak. Basketball was a productive way to occupy myself. The freedom of my neighborhood let me practice in private on empty courts or go to the park to play with older kids. I grew comfortable with making my own choices and with time alone. As much as I have anger about my father's absence, I'm also glad for it. Had he been involved, things might have been far worse for me. I look at Todd and what he went through alone, getting more criticism than encouragement, and I can't help but feel grateful.

But the anger I had for my father was a smoldering one. It burned slow and deep inside me, a constant source of heat that rarely flared into a fire that I couldn't handle. I know I wanted how I felt about him to be different. I wanted him to love me for who I was and to see me as a person with my own ideas. I didn't need him to love basketball or any of my dreams, but I desperately needed his approval for having dreams at all. Instead, there was just unworthiness, a persistent feeling that nothing I did mattered much to him, and by implication, the world. It was my love for him, and the impossibility of feeling it in return, that made him the first person in my life that I loved and hated at the same time.

I've always feared that if I released all of my anger toward my father at once, I'd lose myself. My feelings for him have been like a tightly leashed monster, a dragon by my side, snarling with me and for me throughout my life. It was a dragon I knew how to feed and hide. That dragon would help fuel me to practice and train, and I discovered anger was an energy I could use to help me do hard work. But to let go of that leash, to put the anger in charge of its own choices, would reveal it was more powerful than I could control. I've been working throughout my life to let go of that monster without it consuming me at the same time.

Yet I've wondered in bad times, like this new affair where my father seems lost, that perhaps if he saw the power of that naked rage, he'd understand and see who I was for the first time. It would wake him up. It's a wishful, magical thought of a child. I wanted a formula for my father, a way to figure out what to put in to get out what I needed. I never imagined that for some people, including those in my family, no such formula exists. People are not vending machines. We don't all make sense to each other or even ourselves.

I never told my father about what my mother's boyfriends were like during the separation. It was a strange thing as a child to have other men in my life, men who weren't strictly friends or family of my parents. But my father never asked me about it, and I've felt telling him those stories seemed too cruel, as he'd take it as an attack rather than a way to understand his son.

When I was nine, my mother dated a man named Jerry. Unlike the other handful of men she'd dated, he moved into our house. I recall him being nice. Of course, Jerry and my mother had their arguments, and Todd saw far more of his deficiencies than my younger eyes did, but I was happy to have a man in the house again. It felt good to get attention from a man, however small and insignificant it was, like a pat on the head or a smile when he saw me enter the room.

I remember once, before I went to bed, I ran into what had been my parents' bedroom and hopped up on the bed where Jerry was. I leaned in on his shoulder, as far as I could reach, and kissed him on the cheek. I did it instinctively. I had love to give, and it went to the only man who was around. I remember how foreign the stubble of his beard felt on my cheek. Had I never kissed my own father this way? Had I betrayed my father in this moment, embracing a man who was taking his place? Or was it my father's own fault, like the day I greeted him at the screen door to our house, for putting this situation in motion? It's a curious memory. It has never resolved into a simple explanation or reason. The physical sensation of that act was strange and new, as many things happening in my life were at that time, and perhaps that's why it's a memory that has lasted more than thirty years.

In that moment, though, I remember being very happy. I went to my bed smiling and feeling good about everything. Perhaps the whole family had a good evening that night and everything in the world seemed to be in the right place. Beneath any level of consciousness, I assumed this man would be my stepfather, that he would be in my life for a long time, and I welcomed the idea. And I remember how he disappeared when my mother broke up with him and how I never saw him again. My father and Jerry were two very different men, but the results were the same. Two people leaving. Zero explanations. Many doubts.

The seeds of my independence grew from this pattern of men entering and leaving my life. Todd would be distant in my life too for a time. As a teenager I was a graceless winner who had surpassed him in sports. Todd took the heat that would have gone to my father had he been involved enough to be the person I tested myself against. I rejected Todd as I rejected everyone in those adolescent years, seeing my needs for relationships as a weakness, having learned implicitly that to be a man was to be alone.

I've wondered what life would have been like if my mother had never taken my father back, if she had stayed a single parent and made her way on her own. I know for certain we'd have been hurt financially. It would have been hard for her, or anyone with three young children, to make ends meet. I wouldn't have been able to afford going away to college, and without my father's financial support, it would have taken far more courage to leave the orbit of NYC. As much as I love my hometown, I'm grateful I left it. The opportunities I found by moving away define me as much as where I'm from.

But if my father had never returned, I'd have been protected from the lie of our family. I wouldn't have absorbed the pretense that we were a functional unit or the empty faith that he was fully present and committed to us. I've fantasized about the family in *This Boy's Life* by

Tobias Wolfe, where he writes about how his young mother never feared leaving bad situations. She'd move with her young boy from town to town and man to man, unafraid of the future. I'm sure Wolfe suffered in his own way from their lack of stability. My father's return at least anchored us to a place and a pattern for the rest of my childhood, as broken as it was. But I can't help wondering what I'd be like if I had been born to a parent who felt free in the world, who led me out into life instead of trying to protect me from it.

The separation affected the three of us kids differently. Todd and I were diminished by the separation and the years that came after my parents reunited. When the separation happened, my mother had her own wounds and new responsibilities to tend to, and there was less of her attention to go around. My brother and I were too weak, stupid, or good-natured to play the situation to our advantage. Our sister Tracy, on the other hand, saw the angles and used them. I don't think less of her for this; I just wish she'd have clued us in so we could have benefited too. A minor tragedy of that time was how little any of us siblings talked about what was happening and how we could help each other. We were each on our own, divided in the same ways our parents had been.

Tracy was four years older than me and two years younger than Todd, the middle child in age, and as the only girl, in gender. I can't say if being in the middle was the cause of her problems, but it didn't help. She was a difficult child. Even during my childhood, my relationship with her went through many phases, some good and some bad, but they were all punctuated by her rages. She possessed volcanic emotions, crying and yelling over small matters and taking outrage at small, unintended slights.

There were years when she and I played well together nearly every day. We used to love to bake desserts, taking over the kitchen to make cookies, cupcakes, and our own made-up creations. Tracy was patient with me. Being four years older, she was in charge and wielded her control kindly. As I love to cook now as an adult, I can't dismiss the significance of that first exposure to cooking. When I was in junior high school, Tracy would cut my hair or drive me places I needed to go, which was kind and sisterly of her. She could be sweet, except when she wasn't.

Once when I was young enough that I was still playing baseball, she was in our garage with a friend looking for something fun to do. She asked if she could borrow my glove and baseball, and I said no. She took the baseball bat from the wall and hit me with it. I cried of course, not because she'd hit me particularly hard, but from the shock of being attacked in this way. Todd had a thousand chances to bully me or push me around, yet he never did.

She didn't babysit me often, but one night she did. After it got dark outside, she quietly turned off all the lights in the house. From down the hallway to my room she pretended to be possessed by the devil. She made ghostly sounds and stared straight at me as she slowly walked down the hall. I begged her to stop, asking and asking not to play this strange game. But she didn't give in. Something in her wanted to know about her power over me and what she could do with it. She never did this again, in part because it didn't work. I already knew to be afraid of her. Years later she'd apologize for that night, and I accepted it, but I never forgot it either. It was so unlike anything else I'd experienced in that house.

Tracy's emotions had powers mine didn't have. They took her to places I don't think even she wanted to go. Perhaps she'd had psychological issues that needed attention before the separation, and everything that happened in our family made them worse. Or maybe the separation itself was the cause. All I'm certain of is that she lost control of herself often. Throughout her teenage years, she'd often storm off from the dinner table to her room in tears. Once there, she'd scream and yell, pounding the walls with her fists or lying on the bed to kick the walls.

My parents never knew what to do, and I wouldn't have known either. It was a different era of parenting, without the accepted arsenal of books, programs, and medications for psychological problems children are offered today. My father, as was his way, did nothing. It was often his remarks, sharper for Tracy than for Todd or me, that set her off, and it was beyond his comprehension that he was the cause. Sometimes he'd make a joke at her expense after she left, but while none of us laughed, we did nothing to help either.

My mother took more responsibility than the rest of us combined. Sometimes she'd walk to Tracy's door to talk to her. Other times, she left Tracy alone to calm down. Eventually Tracy exhausted herself, we'd patch things up, and then repeat the same routine a few weeks later. We were all afraid of Tracy in one way or another, afraid of being the person that awakened her rage, or fearful of being around when it surfaced. I knew from a young age that my father and Tracy were dangerous, and Todd and Mom were safe.

The tragedy of my family might have simply been that my mother, as the swing vote, invested the most in our volatile side. Tracy and Howard frequently had dramas, grievances, and episodes, far more than Todd or I ever did. As the years went on, she doubled and redoubled her commitments to them, motivated by a mother's love but also by the need to feel needed, something they offered her in infinite supply. As Todd and I moved away from the family, the trio that remained in Queens stacked their house of cards higher and higher. When it came crumbling down, it may have been too much for my father to bear, driving him to flee his family for a second time.

I moved to Seattle in 1994, taking the first job I was offered after college. Todd moved out of the house in 1992 to an apartment in Hicksville, Long Island. It was only Tracy who stayed behind. She went away to Albany

University for a semester but dropped out after struggling with rowdy roommates and the challenges of independence. After returning home, she finished college and went to work but stayed in the same bedroom she'd slept in all of her life. I was still in high school at the time, and watching Todd and Tracy struggle to find their way only fueled my desire to leave as quickly as I could.

When Tracy got married two years later, she and her husband moved into the downstairs apartment beneath my parents' house. Previously, my parents had rented it out to strangers, but they were happy to help their daughter by renting it to her instead. When Tracy had her second child, my parents traded places with her, moving into the downstairs apartment. Todd married too and moved up to a town in Connecticut a few hours away. When Tracy was pregnant with her third child, my mother and father decided it was time to make big changes and finally leave NYC. The surprise was they wanted Tracy and her young family to move with them, and Tracy and her husband agreed. They decided to buy neighboring plots in the same town where my brother now lived. With my strong ideas about independence, their plan seemed mad, and I told them so. No one would grow if they stayed together, and they, like all of us, had growing they needed to do. Maybe it could be a healthy choice if they parted for a time and then reunited, but that was not the plan. But my opinion was easy to dismiss. My voice then was filled with judgment, fitting the reputation I'd earned as the arrogant son and brother who lived very far away.

My parents built the house they'd always wanted, a home superior to their dreams because this one would have their grandchildren next door. The two planned houses had hardwood floors, great rooms with gloriously high ceilings, and acres of property stretching out into the forests in the backyards. It was my parents' vision for the last home they'd ever own. As the house neared completion, they felt overwhelming pride. Tracy was finally the star of the family, something she'd wanted all her life. In my parents' eyes, she'd transformed from a difficult child into someone special. They saw her as the only child interested in staying so close and so willing to share her children with their grandparents.

While still in Queens planning their move, Tracy's husband opened a bar on Bell Boulevard, two miles up the road from my parents' house. My father generously made this possible by extending loans and making his own investments in the project. I talked to him on the phone about putting money in myself, an act of solidarity for my sister. He told me that while this was thoughtful, it wasn't my risk to take. He said it would make things more complicated between me and Tracy. My father was a smart man, especially where matters of business and money were concerned, so I yielded. But after the phone call, I wondered, wasn't he taking the same risks, or more so, by using his own money? Tracy was not only his daughter, a relationship with a difficult history, but his neighbor and the mother of his grandchildren all wrapped up in one.

By the time my sister and parents moved into their new homes in Connecticut, the bar was in trouble. Bars are tough businesses anywhere, with high rates of failure for even the most experienced businessmen, which they weren't. As it went into decline and soon bankruptcy, tensions grew. I couldn't keep track of who was blaming whom for what. As always, most of what I learned came from Mom. I'd hear fragments of news and plans that would "resolve the matter for good" that never worked. Eventually all the money that went into the business, a sizable fortune, was gone. Tracy's husband found a new job near Connecticut as her family struggled to recover from what had been both a family and financial disaster.

I didn't talk to Tracy often, but even when I did, the conversations were polite and short. I was very bad at returning or initiating phone calls, which made things worse, but even when we spoke, there just wasn't much we were willing to say. Todd and I talked every few months, and we always had plenty to share. We often swapped notes about how Tracy and our parents were doing, piecing together the details each of us had heard independently from Mom. In one conversation, we realized Tracy's situation was a mystery. Were she and her family doing okay? There seemed to be more going on than Mom was willing to share. Instead of guessing with Todd, I decided I should reach out to Tracy directly and ask. Things were different now that we were adults, I thought. We were still in the patterns of the past, and I didn't want that to be the case anymore. I didn't want to depend on my mother to learn about my siblings, or them about me. I was nervous about calling Tracy but decided I was nervous because it was new. I had to take some of my own childhood armor off. I only had one sister, and I owed it to her and myself to try.

I dialed her number a half-dozen times, hanging up each time before it rang. I'd never done this kind of phone call before. I considered emailing instead, but it seemed so impersonal, and cowardly, at the time. Eventually I let the call go through, and I told her what was on my mind. I explained I was worried about her, given how little I knew, yet cared enough to call and say something. It was awkward and uncomfortable, and I lacked the tact these calls require, but she obliged. She told me the details of the bar's closing and how things were now. I understood more about the reality of her life, for better and for worse, than I'd heard from her in years.

But something I said, or the call itself, upset her. When we spoke again the next day, it went horribly wrong. She felt attacked, I felt hurt that she felt attacked, and we spiraled together down to dark places. I yelled, she cried, and soon she yelled back. Thirty years of feelings we'd never shared came violently to the surface. As ugly as it was, it was the most honest conversation I would ever have with my sister. We jumped between the present and the past, with all the resentments, grudges, and judgments that accumulate in families. After an hour, we both hung up in frustration.

After the call, I considered a lesson I'd learned from my father. Sometimes two people willing to fight care more than any number of people not willing to argue at all. As painful as it was to discover, I realized how much Tracy and I cared for each other. We'd failed to express those feelings in a positive way, but we definitely shared something important. The question was: what now?

I regretted some things I'd said, and felt she probably did too. This was an opportunity, a possible break-through, I thought. Mom had taught all of us, through her actions, the importance of reconciliation. People who care about each other should come back the next day to sort out what happened the day before. My father rarely did this, but she pushed him and all of us to try. She taught us to apologize and to be responsible for our behavior. More than anyone else in our family, it was my mother who exemplified what it meant to be present, fair, and loving.

I knew I had to call Tracy the next day and try to reconcile. Maybe, as adults, Tracy and I were ready to progress in our relationship. I felt hopeful about it. We'd revealed so much in that fight, and with cooler minds, there was plenty to explore and learn from. Something important that I needed, reconnecting with a sister I'd been so distant from for so long, was possible. Unlike the first call, I dialed the phone and let it go through the first time.

The surprise was that when I called she didn't answer the phone. I called the next day and the next. I left messages on her answering machine. Finally, after many attempts, her husband answered. I'd never heard him answer the phone before. He spoke plainly and said, "Tracy is not home." I asked when she'd be back, and he said he didn't know. It was a strange moment, the two of us stuck in silence, him not wanting to tell me the truth, and me being too afraid to ask. Over the next days, I kept calling, hoping I'd understood this all wrong, but slowly it sank in that this was no accident. She wasn't talking to me on purpose, and she wanted me to figure this out on my own. Desperate, I asked my mother. She told me, "Yes, Tracy has decided she is not talking to you anymore." I didn't know what to think. Had I missed something? I reviewed my last conversation with her over and over, trying to find something I'd missed. What had I done that justified this?

When I visited my parents' house a few weeks later, I knew I wouldn't see Tracy. I doubted I'd even get to see her children – my niece and nephews. The closer I drove to where my family was, the further away I felt from them. My parents were decidedly neutral about the situation, leaving me to sort it out for myself. It was a strange trip, a new kind of family ambivalence. When I arrived, I put my bags down in my parents' guest bedroom and looked out the window. I saw my sister's yard, her children's bicycles and soccer balls left out across the grass. I watched as her dog Cody went out with her children to play. At night when I went to bed, I'd see their lights on, knowing inside was a part of my family that wanted nothing to do with me for reasons I didn't understand.

In the months that followed, I sent Tracy flowers for her birthday and emails every few months, asking for a chance to reconcile. My father and mother advised me to reach out, and I took their advice. My messages were brief, as accepting as I could be, but honest about how sad and confused I was. They made little difference. It would be another year before we'd talk briefly on the phone for the first time. By then I'd accepted how limited our relationship was going to be, probably forever. She was a mystery to me, but one everyone else tolerated. I took it as enough that I could see her and play with her children when I visited.

On one visit, I taught all her kids – Tara, Aaron, Gavin, and Aidan – how to make paper airplanes, just like Todd had shown me. We went out to their deck to see who could throw them farthest out into the yard. I tried to focus on the kids. I didn't want them not to know one of their uncles because of something I'd done. I didn't want to repeat my failures with Tracy with others I cared about. In the years that followed, I'd spend many hours with unanswered questions on my mind. I didn't think of it then, but perhaps Tracy had learned something from our father about leaving people behind.

Five years later, in 2011, Tracy and her family secretly moved away from Connecticut. She did it much in the same way as she had treated me: leaving without a forwarding address, a phone number, or an explanation. My parents and Tracy had stopped talking for periods of time, their relationship decaying with each passing year. The grandchildren became the primary bond they shared. My mother discovered Tracy's final decision to leave by chance. One ordinary day, she walked down to their mailbox on the street to get the morning mail. As she stood there, she couldn't help but notice the "for sale" sign outside her daughter's house. There hadn't been enough of a relationship left for Tracy to feel the need to say goodbye, or to let my parents kiss their grandchildren one last time.

When I visited my parents in June of 2012, before anyone knew of Howard's second affair, I had high hopes. Tracy had moved away only a few months before. I'd talked to Mom and Todd about it individually, but never as a family. Tracy's departure from the entire family, not just me, put things in a new light. Maybe my struggles with her hadn't been my fault. Perhaps there was something deeper at work than what I had or hadn't said in a phone call those many years ago. The distance I'd felt from the family all these years might now change into something else, something better.

I imagined us having a dinner like we used to have on our better nights in Queens. We'd pick up a pizza, get some Entenmann's doughnuts for dessert, and have a long, wonderful discussion. As sad as Tracy's departure was, our family was good at dark humor. This could be a new beginning for us. I looked forward to it for weeks before I arrived. I asked Todd in advance if he could come over to our parents' house the first night so we could have our family chat as soon as possible.

I was excited on that night. I remember sitting down at my parents' pale wood table, just past the stone island in their kitchen. This kitchen was three times the size of the one I'd grown up with in Queens. From where I sat, I saw their living room with ceilings high enough to fit a basketball hoop inside. Up the stairs, just past the living room's wide couches, was the stairway up to the empty bedrooms, ones that had often been reserved for my sister's children and their friends to sleep over, but might never be occupied by them again.

Everyone was friendly and happy to see me, as they always were when I came to visit. We joked around in the way we usually did, led by me and Todd making each other laugh, and Mom and my father following along. After an hour, I was surprised no one had brought up the big topic for discussion. I assumed now that we were together everyone would want to talk about Tracy's departure, but perhaps it was just me who had any interest at all. I forced the issue, as it was too important, to me, not to.

"Oh, you want to talk about that," my mother said with a sarcastic smile.

But no one else spoke. We were like a table of strangers forced to sit together at a restaurant, staring into space, lost in feelings we didn't want to share. I had my thoughts but didn't feel right about offering them first. I wanted to see what my family thought and how they'd talk about it independent of what I had to say. But the silence continued. Perhaps we'd waited far too long, or I was wrong, and talking about this at all was a mistake.

I pushed harder, and Mom and Todd shared their general dismay. It was just a sad thing, they said. I offered that Tracy's events of the past, how she had stopped talking to me for over a year, had new significance now, and they agreed. But this wasn't enough for me. I'd hoped for some kind of validation in all this, a relief from the past. Howard had been the quietest of all so far, brooding as he sometimes did over conversations. His mind was elsewhere. I couldn't tell if the darkness over him was about Tracy or something else.

I asked him directly, as he was the only one who hadn't spoken. "So Dad, how do you feel about what's happened?"

He had no choice but to reply, even if he didn't want to. I'd stirred up something in him, a feeling he didn't want to express but which was powerful enough to come out on its own. His face filled up with emotion, his cheeks red and his intense eyes open wide, looking past us all and into the empty living room. His voice climbed in power as he said, "Maybe it was my fault, okay? I shouldn't have tried to play God!"

And that last word was a word that said this conversation was over. Disappointed, I let it go. It was just my first day, and I expected I'd have another chance to talk to him, and with everyone, about it again. Maybe I could ask the question differently, framed in a way he'd find easier to answer. Or perhaps what I wanted could only be found in talking to Todd and Mom without him around. On that night, I went to bed in the same guest bedroom in my parents' new house that I'd slept in before. I looked out the same window I'd looked out on previous visits and saw the house that used to be my sister's. There was a new kind of sorrow looking out that window. My parents had invested so much to put these two houses together, and now, what was left? It was inconceivable, looking out that window on that sad night, that my family had a larger crisis brewing. I'd never have guessed that that night would be the last time the four of us would ever be in the same room together.

THREE

....

YELLOWSTONE

Who knows why my sister left? Who knows why my father had a second affair? I've spent hundreds of hours thinking about these questions, talking to Mom and my brother, searching for answers, reading books on family psychology, and talking to experts; there are no definitive answers. There is no one reason anyone does anything. Like the mysteries of why some memories stay with us and some don't, the hardest choices we make don't come with simple reasons. Maybe it's a side effect of our dependence on memory, and the craving our brains have for everything to fit into simple stories, that we demand simple reasons for everything. Even if my sister and my father had one clear reason why they think they did what they did, I'm not certain I'd believe it. There are only patterns and vocabularies, things we learn from those around us that we emulate.

I see the circle of abandonment – one person cutting ties from others – rippling through my family in wave after wave. My grandmother abandoned my father, or at least he feels she did. My father abandoned us, or at least I feel he did. I abandoned my family to move to Seattle. My sister abandoned me and then everyone all at once. And then my father completed the circle by leaving for a second time. It's just in my family's language. We're good at being alone and separate from each other.

The last email I received from my father was in July of 2012. It was a month after my visit and our last family gathering. In that email he'd written, with uncharacteristic optimism, "My ears are open." My honest reply met no response. He returned to Australia, as he'd always planned, but made no contact with me. Every few weeks afterwards, I sent my father a new email. They were short. I asked why I hadn't heard from him and for him to explain himself.

From: Scott Berkun
Date: Tuesday, July 10, 2012 at 1:39 PM
To: Howard
Subject: Re: Your legacy with the Berkun family

I haven't heard from you in a week. I hope you're doing well.

From: Scott Berkun
Date: Friday, August 3, 2012 at 9:43 AM
To: Howard
Subject: Re: Your legacy with the Berkun family

You haven't answered my last two emails. Almost a month ago I wrote you and you haven't responded to me in any way. I deserve better.

They were hopeless missives. I didn't expect a response; mostly I wanted to feel better for doing something. When you're lost at sea and running out of supplies, you fire your bright red signal flares into the night sky simply because you can. There is nothing left to try, so you do it. Being my father's son had often felt like being lost at sea, but this was new. There were no excuses for him to hide behind anymore. He couldn't pretend, by merely standing next to my mother, that he had a relationship with me. It was disturbing to compare my relationship with Tracy to my relationship with him. They were more alike than I'd realized. Perhaps their many fights over the years had been based on their inability to relate to someone so like themselves.

No person deserves to be rejected from their family without an explanation, or even perhaps with one. But I was foolish to think there was anything on his mind about me specifically. That's the hook of insecurity: you take someone else's dysfunction to mean more about you than it does about them. When you ask, "How could you do this?" enough times of someone and never like the answer, it means you need to ask the question of yourself. My father had lied to everyone for months. He betrayed my mother in the worst way, and she had been his best friend, the only friend he'd ever had in his life.

There was no one else for him to lean on. If he could do this to her after the life they'd shared, he was capable of doing worse to me. His behavior told me everything I needed to know. Yet here I was, still thinking about him again and again and again.

Perhaps I wrote him out of guilt, the old guilt from having moved away. There was also the need to hold on to reality. I needed reminders that the feeling of loss I felt confirmed, rather than denied, my sanity. After I sent each email, I felt relieved. It helped me remember this is something that happens. Then a week would go by, then two, then four, and I'd accumulate this lingering sense of dread that I needed to do something. And when I did, there was relief again. With each email, I worked through the same loop of emotional logic:

- Yes, Scott, your father is actively not talking to you.
- Yes, he is disappearing again.
- And yes, he is behaving in much the way Tracy did when she stopped talking to you for a year.
- No, there is no problem with your email account. There will be no texts, no phone calls, no telegraphs, and no carrier pigeons. He will not avail himself of any conveyances of information, as the problem is not the machines; the problem is the man.

I read through my twenty years of journals, looking to the past to help me understand myself in the present. I wondered: How did what I remember feeling on important days match how I had actually felt on those days? A journal is a time travel machine. It records what you were thinking five, ten, or twenty years ago. I discovered events and feelings and stories I'd forgotten long ago, but now that I was reading them, they were entirely familiar. Others I had no recollection of, the journal being the only record of their existence. The big surprise was just how many times I'd reached out to my father – and how the results each time were largely the same:

- **1992**: When my father lost his job, I wrote him a letter. I'd had a rough year of failure myself, transferring between three colleges in three semesters. I felt I was enough of an adult that I could reach out to him as one. The letter was positive. I told him failure could be transformative, as mine had been. I sent the letter. He briefly thanked me for it and said nothing more.
- **June 1994**: I talked to everyone in my family about our relationships. At twenty-two, I wanted a new start. For my father, I told him how much happier he seemed since he lost his job and started his own business. He was much easier to be around than when I was growing up. I told him I hadn't

felt like I knew him until now. He thanked me, and I moved on.

- **October 1998**: During a visit, I talked to Mom and Dad about the good and bad of my childhood. I had more to say to him than her. They both listened, but mostly she and I talked.
- **May 2000**: I confronted my father directly about the past. It led to the only trip we'd ever taken alone together, to Yellowstone.
- **Summer 2007**: I wrote him a letter out of the blue. There was no agenda other than sharing my dreams for my life. It ended with me asking him questions that were on my mind: What is a great man? What is a good life? What lessons should I be trying to learn? He never answered.

I'm surprised by this list. I didn't realize how many offers I'd made to my father. Why had I kept trying? What wasn't I learning? To paraphrase Kierkegaard, we live life forward but understand it only by looking backward. Each act I took was a momentary expression of my wish to have a better relationship with him. They were spaced years apart, and when I did these things, I didn't see them as part of a pattern. With the exception of Yellowstone, few of these acts required much risk, and I had little to lose by trying. But now I'm fascinated by how they all fit together.

I believe that with people I care for I have to make new offers now and then. People can change, but relationships fall into old patterns, and old patterns in families, often guarded in the name of tradition, hide many problems. For a relationship to grow or even just maintain itself, someone has to put new energy in from time to time, changing a rule or shifting a habit. It could be an unexpected invitation to a baseball game or a surprise phone call for no particular reason at all. The odds might be low of something changing, as the other person might not want anything to change, but low odds are better than no odds at all.

I remember hoping for, but not expecting, responses from my father. In those post-college years, I started to understand who I was and who I wanted to be. I realized I wanted to be the kind of man who reached out. I wanted the love that I felt to be more than the abstraction it is for so many men. I hated the cliché of people saying, "You know I love you, right?" – a backhanded, rhetorical question that has only one expected answer. It's a statement usually made by someone who realizes they may have hurt the other person's feelings. But the only reasonable response, an answer I've never heard anyone say, is: "I don't know. The only time you tell me is at times like this."

I wanted love to be more obvious, more direct, and overt, more my mother's kind of love rather than a platitude we say in safety but are terrified to express. I didn't know how to do this well, of course; I was my father's son, but I was my mother's son too. I'd been learning from my wife Jill how narrow my view of love was, and I was committed to working on it. Writing personal letters was an obvious place for me to invest in my end of the relationships I was born with, including with my father.

But seeing the list disturbed me. It was like I was stuck in a loop of my own making, repeating the same pointless tasks again and again. Like the film *Groundhog Day*, I seemed stuck in the same place, not learning what I needed to learn to move on. It made me reconsider the very idea of writing this book. Couldn't this be just another commitment of time to thinking of him, in that writing about that loop was also continuing it? Did I really do these things primarily for myself and for healthy reasons? Or was I holding on to a childhood dream of discovering, as if by magic, that one day, like Luke Skywalker, I'd get what I'd always needed from him?

Todd had an epiphany that changed my life. He suggested one night, while our father was on his second trip to Australia, that we've had it backward all along. Howard wasn't trying to escape; he was always somewhere else. All his distance, his nights at the racetrack and the casinos, his first affair and separation, were all an attempt to find a true home – something he never found. This Australian affair wasn't an anomaly. Instead, it was a continuation of his search for a place where he belonged. He was never here. He had always been a ghost. His second affair was the continuation of the first, a deep longing for another way to live. His long email about his failed life fits this theory well.

This discovery seems obvious now. I feel stupid for not realizing it years ago. But this is the power of family. I was blind to what any outsider might have seen. Just as a fish is the last to see the water, perhaps a child is the last to see their parents. Moving to Seattle had made me an outsider to my family, and for years, I wanted back in. That desire gave me an additional blind spot, making it harder to see any of them for who they were.

Regardless of when I should have known, what my brother said rippled through my mind. Insight feels magical – the sudden shift of a hundred discordant thoughts into a single line that snaps tightly together. I'd always felt my father's inexplicable absence, but now I saw there were two ghosts at work: one my father had made for his family, and the one I had made for him. I'd cultivated a hate not just for his limitations, but how they paled in comparison to the ideal father I'd invented. I kept trying to reach out to him not because of who he was, but because of who I was. Now I could see it was never about him; it was about me. And I was an adult now. The only way this was going to change was if I changed.

I can't express how sad it made me to admit I'd spent a lifetime arguing with a man who wasn't even paying attention. The metaphor of a ghost was only partially accurate. He wasn't haunting me. He was barely inter-ested in me. I'd been reaching out all my life to a disin-terested man, or a man too broken to respond. He had been the worst thing about my life, but I didn't know how to accept the notion that I barely registered in his.

For my part, I know I feared regret, and that fear fueled my choices. I wanted to be able to say, on the day he or I was about to die, that I had fought for something. That regardless of what had built the wall, I'd swung every sledgehammer I could find against it. Even if no one but me would care, I'd be able to point to the scratches and the scars in the bricks I'd hit and know that I tried. Even with Tracy, even if I had caused what happened, I don't regret having tried. I wanted to give my father many chances to listen from the other side, however slim those chances were. But as his departure to Australia reached its second month, I knew the time for change, if it had been possible at all, was fading.

While Howard was in Australia, my mother was sadder than I'd ever seen her. She was like how she had been during the first separation, when she'd quietly disappear to the basement to smoke cigarettes. With three kids, she'd been able to bury some of her sadness behind the work of taking care of us. There'd always been something to do or someone who needed help with something. For this second affair, after Tracy's departure, my mother was left with nothing. There were no grandkids next door. There were no couples' dinners out with my mother's friends. It was a despair I couldn't imagine, to have bet her life on one man, and given him a second chance, only to have him disappear again.

As an adult, I'd sometimes think about how the triad of Todd, Mom, and me were the best part of the family. We were the most stable, the most open, and the most loving. But somehow my father and Tracy were always at the center. Since I lived 2400 miles away, it was hard to explore the idea, but perhaps Howard making his way out of the family would make the three of us stronger. The two most difficult people in the family would be gone. We could be the family we might have been had my parents never reunited thirty years ago.

I spoke to my mother at least once a week. She, Todd, and I developed a makeshift alliance, more deeply connected than ever, bonded by my father's absence. I felt closer to both of them than I had in years. But as the weeks of the crisis became months, my mother's choice became harder to comprehend. When Howard returned from his second trip to Australia, she, to my surprise, let him stay in their house. He was undecided about his future but wanted to stay with her while he was back in the United States. She'd told me that since he'd left, she'd slept with a baseball bat in the bed next to her, not for safety, but just not to feel alone. She'd shared her bed with him for most of her life, and his absence had been hard to bear. I couldn't imagine sharing a house with him after what he'd done, but I was not my mother. There was not a moment's hesitation from her about letting him stay.

I warned her not to trust him, not out of spite or anger, but because of his confusion. Part of the reason

Howard hadn't found the confidence to tell Mom, or anyone, about the affair was that he was deeply lost. As a seventy-year-old man, he didn't know what he wanted from his life any more than he had when he was fifty or twenty-five. It's hard to know what you want from life if you don't know who you are.

I wonder when he was happiest in his life. What memories could I summon of him in his full glory, happiest and most fulfilled? He was a restrained man. He didn't celebrate well. He didn't go to parties or drink beers with friends, since he had no friends. He stayed within a well-defined pattern of life, a pattern defined by his mother or mine, that, regardless of how it made him feel, he followed with little visible hesitation. Perhaps his happiest times were at the blackjack table. He'd stay at casinos for hours, staring at blackjack hand after hand from six p.m. until the early morning hours. He told me once that it was meditation for him, an activity that freed him from any concerns in this world.

His weekly trips during my childhood to the race-track fit the same pattern, as did his love for trading stocks, staring for hours into the cold, angular lines of stock charts. He had the air of Asperger Syndrome about him, or maybe just social phobia, struggling at times with social interactions yet loving deep concentration in math and numbers. Perhaps he was happy there, or maybe it was just an escape. He often wanted us to come with him, but none of us enjoyed these things the way he did. I remember as a kid spending long Saturday nights in the grandstands at Roosevelt Raceway or Yonkers Raceway. He'd stare out at horses on the track through his binoculars while Tracy and I played with the discarded ticket stubs we found on the floor, looking for winning tickets that had been left behind. We were accessories; he just wanted us around while he did what he liked to do.

Socrates would probably say the only way to ensure you're not an asshole is to assume you are one. Shakespeare wrote, "To thine own self be true... and thou canst not then be false to any man." But what if you're false to yourself? What then? As I was learning from my father, if you're false to yourself, then anything is possible. But self-awareness is fragile. If you are an asshole, and a friend tells you you're being an asshole, you'll probably stop being friends with them. Provided you have the gumption to continually end relationships, you can go through life never confronting the reality of who you are. Once you abandon someone, you no longer hear their arguments, no matter how valid they were. And as it is with our malleable memories, soon your mind will, all on its own, replace the critiques that cut to the bone with paper tigers that justify your every action.

For a long time, I'd taken my father as a cautionary tale. I've known I have to keep people around me who will tell me things I don't want to hear. It's something even my father has said, in passing, as advice to my brother and me: "It's your best friend who will tell you things that hurt sometimes, not your enemy." But as my father and the history of our greatest philosophers proves, good philosophy is easy to talk about and hard to practice. Nietzsche, Kant, and dozens of others struggled to maintain marriages, friendships, jobs, and relationships of all kinds. My father certainly had wisdom, but his ego was far more powerful.

I knew telling my mother not to trust my father wasn't what she wanted to hear, but I didn't know who else would be honest with her. I told her I was worried about him taking their retirement savings with him to Australia. I didn't see how that wasn't a possibility. She defended him. She said he wouldn't do that to her. I asked her: "How can you trust him, given that three months ago you'd have told me he'd never cheat on you again?" Trust is fragile. Trust is faith. From my own marriage, I know that when you plant a seed of doubt, it grows faster and with more power than many relationships can recover from.

Betrayal bleeds backward into the past, putting doubts and worries into what were once wonderful memories of connection. Betrayal is poison not just for the present, but for the past and the future too. But wishful thinking has similar powers. If we need something desperately enough, we'll invent reasons to look past the facts. Our emotions drive our intellects far more than we admit. It's people who think they are the most rational who are the least. They're blind to the powerful undercurrents of emotions selecting for them which thoughts to have and which facts to consider or ignore.

In July of 2012, things grew worse. My parents had had long-standing plans to buy a winter home in Florida. New Yorkers are notorious for aging into snowbirds – people who leave the Northeast for warmer climates in the winter. As an act of independence, my mother decided she wanted the house regardless of what my father decided about his future with her. I liked this plan as she explained it to me. Making decisions is empowering, and when we're weak, it's often through exercising what power we do still have that we learn to become stronger again. The twist was my mother asked him to drive down to Florida with her to buy a house. To sum up the absurdity of this sentence, here is the rundown:

- My father's second affair, with a woman he'd only known online for a few months, involved flying to Australia as part of a lie to my mother.
- My mother had to force him to admit to the affair.
- She learned he had already planned to return to Australia.
- He made clear he did not know what he wanted to do.
- In between trips to Australia, my father stayed with my mother.
- They were buying a new house together in Fort Lauderdale in the middle of the worst crisis of their marriage.

The drive from Connecticut to Fort Lauderdale is twenty hours long, the equivalent of ten full-length movies back to back with no intermissions. I love road trips, but the notion of sitting inches away from someone who had recently broken my heart was hard to imagine. I tried to guess what the conversations in that car must have been like. Would they talk about sightseeing in Australia? Or how the U.S. economy was doing these days? I thought about the cliché of passengers rearranging deck chairs on the Titanic: how we all do what's familiar, despite its uselessness, when we are truly panicked. But then I realized I might have it all backward. Maybe they weren't in denial at all.

Perhaps this madness, this capacity to deny, was the way their relationship had been all along, and I was just too blind to notice. It could be their relationship had always been twisted, intimate and distant, sane and insane. My father had called it a cockeyed marriage, which I didn't like to hear as a justification for his choices, but maybe he was right. I'd understood for years how broken my father was, but I realized now that my mother had to be broken too to fit together with him so willingly. The car ride wasn't an exception; she'd been on this ride with him her whole life and still wasn't looking for a way to get off.

Codependence is a cycle. Each person needs the other badly, in the way an alcoholic needs another drink. When one takes a drink of the other, just like a glass of wine, it feels good. It covers certain holes, allowing them, in moments, to be forgotten, but does not fill them. My father and mother love each other for that feeling and hate each other for the same reason. They crave the feeling of their holes fading away but know it's the other person who holds them back from who they'd become if they didn't have those holes at all. It's a cycle that never ends, like a snake eating its tail. My father needs to be mothered, and my mother needs someone to care for, and neither one can escape.

And codependence is a disease that spreads, as each link in the chain welcomes more. My sister was just the next link for my parents. Had I not moved away, I might have been another. Their support for Tracy, moving to neighboring houses in Connecticut, bound them and their deep issues together. As destructive as Tracy's departure was, it was her escape. If there's hope for her, it began the day she decided to go out on her own. Tracy broke the triangle that helped keep my parents' family together and held it back from growing. My father's affair was, like my sister's departure, an attempt to escape. But now, whether for guilt, fear, hope, or love, my mother and father were still working together. They found a small home in Fort Lauderdale, bought some furniture, and made it their own. After driving back to Connecticut, my father left for Australia for a third time, planning to stay there for three months, the longest period of time his visa would allow.

That summer fell into familiar patterns: silence from my father, silence from my sister, and long phone calls with my brother and mother. To my relief, I thought about the situation less and less. It didn't occupy my dreams and spare moments anymore. My mother seemed more confident in her new life. She was always a reader, studying anything that was on her mind, and this crisis was no different. She read books about the psychology of affairs, about narcissistic personality disorder, which she believed my father suffered from, and more. In our family, she was always the learner, always curious, and that's how I know I'm my mother's son. I'm the same way: always reading and asking questions. To see her use her emotions as fuel for discovery made me believe she was finding her way, not the way she wanted, but a better way nonetheless.

Then in October of 2012, while my father was still in Australia, there was an unfathomable request. Mom asked me and Todd to reach out to our father. He was returning soon to Connecticut, and she wanted us, the children he'd ignored over these last months, to welcome him home. She explained that her friend, who is a therapist, thought this was a good idea. She wanted us to let him know he was still loved by us. How could she even ask such a thing, I thought. That *he* was still loved by *us*?

Whenever someone says their therapist thinks something is a good idea, I immediately wonder what they told their therapist. The best therapist in the world can only respond to what their patient tells them. If the patient omits a fact or chooses one perspective over another, the therapist can't know. Self-knowledge is self-knowledge. If you lie to your therapist, if you paint for them a picture of wishful images, you're lost and always will be lost. You can lead a therapist, or any expert, to any answer you want to hear if you lie to yourself well enough. There are some problems only you can save yourself from.

Mom understood all too well how I felt about Howard, how disgusted I was by his choices, and how little care I felt he had for anyone but himself. We'd spent hours on the phone sharing horror stories of our pasts with him. That was all forgotten to her now. The request made me a pawn. I was a chip to play, and she was desperate enough to play all the ones she had. And there were more requests. My mother planned a family reunion and asked if I'd come. I told her yes, but only if Howard wasn't there. She was surprised. I had to explain how he was currently behaving as the antithesis of family, and the request went away.

The fifth Commandment of the Bible says to honor thy father and mother. It's a declaration of respect for the unique function two people have in our lives, as they are the people who gave us life. But when they gave us life, they didn't know who we were yet. No one did. It's a gift given to a stranger. The bond of a child to a parent is unique, but it's not absolute. The fifth commandment doesn't say why or under what conditions a particular father or mother is no longer worthy of being honored, which leads many to assume there aren't any. That's the problem with commandments. They're offered as self-evident with no recourse and no amendments. When loopholes are discovered, which every following of every religion eventually finds, they are justified and popularized. Unlike the U.S. Constitution, which had a built-in system for upgrades, the Ten Commandments were etched in stone with the presumption that they'd be perfect forever.

In George Carlin's critique of the Ten Commandments, he says, in reference to the fifth commandment, "Obedience and respect should not be automatic. They should be earned. They should be based on the parent's performance." I agree with him, and I think, to some degree, we all do. There are unspoken conditions where parental respect is lost: physical abuse of children, using children for slave labor, or even serious emotional neglect. Most countries have laws protecting children from documented abuses, and for good reason. But what about for adult children?

When I've told people about the drama in my family and how my parents' choices have hurt me, I've often heard, "But it's your father," or "It's your mother." The collective belief in honoring parents runs so deep that it transcends the decencies we expect from neighbors or strangers on a sidewalk. It denies the mathematics of mental illness, that even if one percent of all adults have narcissistic personality disorder or suffer from severe schizophrenia, some of those people have children, and for those children, the normal boundaries of parental relationships do not apply.

But I do understand the sentiment. I will always feel a debt to my parents and will help them when I can. But there are limits. There are certain things I'd no longer be willing to do for my parents depending on what they'd done to me. Telling lies and treating family members only with silence are all things that break trust, the core of any relationship. My father's grace period for his choices had been closing for months. My generosity toward my mother, who I saw as the victim of the pair, went further. But now her innocence was ending too. This was no longer just something that had happened to her; she was now an active participant in the present.

I wanted my mother to get what she needed. If she wanted him to come back, regardless of my opinions, I wanted to help her if I could. But the specifics were an old game I did not like. It reminded me of being pushed to go help my father paint the railing when I was a child – a nudge to cover up something broken, to gloss over something wrong. She was waving a magical wand of denial over feelings in the family she wanted to pretend were not there. But these were my feelings, and unlike in these childhood dramas, now I was an adult. I told her I thought it was wrong of her to even ask. My relationship with him was my own, and this was a manipulation of it. I offered, if she insisted, that I'd do the absolute minimum. She insisted.

I wrote him an email with a single sentence. It said, "Welcome home." It was all I could say without betraying myself. It bothers me, even now, that I did anything at all. I don't know if it was a mistake or not. It made me feel worse when he replied. I hadn't heard anything from him in months, but this brief note, free of the mess he'd created for himself with me, he answered the same day. He simply said, "Thank you. I hope you're well." I'd wanted to think his silence was because he'd sequestered himself high on some mountain, pondering the deepest existential questions of existence and the universe. Instead, his ears had been wide open all along, but only for what he wanted to hear. And Mom, of all people, knew the kinds of messages Howard liked, something for all my life I'd never figured out for myself.

The one place in my life where I shined for my father was at dinner. We had lively meals in our house, debates and discussions about politics, sports, and history. Often we'd debate the meaning of words or why certain wars were fought or won. We'd pull out dictionaries to look up words or flip through the World Book Encyclopedia to research facts. The dictionary was the biggest one I'd ever seen, so thick that the pages for each letter of the alphabet had a small divot cut out for your finger, making it easier to find your way. I loved the way it felt to fit my fingertip inside, pulling back the thinnest pages I'd ever touched to find the one I needed. The books rarely resolved our debates, teaching me for the first time that knowledge was endless and that good questions led to more questions. Until I experienced the polite tameness of dinner at friends' homes, I didn't know how rare our passionate dinner discussions were.

My father was the star in these debates. He often started them by stating an opinion or fact that provoked the rest of us to respond. He was a master at arguments, knowing just what to say to lure you in, and then, once you were engaged, to turn you around and put you on your heels. He enjoyed it enough that it was fun for all of us, in a way. It was the rare window of his attention where he'd listen, smile, prod, and laugh. Tracy hated these dinner discussions and often left, finding it hard to separate defending a point from defending her identity. Todd and my mother stayed with him, but he'd often find ways to intimidate them out of their positions. I was different, perhaps because I was the youngest or most arrogant or something else. But unlike the rest of the family, I'd keep arguing against him. I rarely gave up.

If I thought I was right, and I did far more often than I was, I'd keep arguing. I'd keep asking questions. And because of my persistence, every now and then I'd catch him in a corner of rhetoric he wasn't prepared for. When it happened, I'd catch a look in his eye, a sideways glance that hid the glimmer of a smile. He'd never say "good job". He'd never say I was smart or that my point was intelligent. In his lifetime of dinner discussions, I doubt he has ever said, declaratively, "That's smart. I've never thought of that before. I need to reconsider my position. Thanks." He'd never explicitly acknowledge that anything interesting had happened. But I'd see that look, and I'd know. Sometimes he'd laugh, not at me, but at something ethereal, as if he'd suddenly found existence itself comical. Laughter was a safe place for him to hide the experience of feeling wrong, a feeling his mother had taught him he shouldn't have. Often he'd change the subject or jump backward in the debate to a point where he had better footing. But I'd know. I'd know I'd scored a point with my old man.

It's no surprise I grew into a young man who loved to argue. I could outlast everyone I knew; none of my friends or coworkers grew up sharing a table with my father. As desperate as I was then to earn those glances from my father, they held a poison. The habit of chasing these thin moments of approval became a central part of my personality. I compulsively needed people I met to think I was smart. I didn't feel comfortable unless I got some acknowledgement, preferably through a debate, that I was right about things. And people who didn't have opinions or didn't want to play the games my father had were boring to me. I didn't respect them. If they offered me other kinds of intimacy, I rejected it, just as my father would have.

My years away in college and in Seattle gave me the gift of distance. I noticed how differently I felt each year when I visited home. A rage in me arose around my father, a desperate need to prove something to him, which I didn't like and didn't understand. I'd try to keep quiet during the debates, telling myself I didn't need to play those old games. I could last a day or two, but by the third day, I'd fall back into who I was and jump into the fray. And then later I'd regret it, but not enough to prevent it from happening next time. Was it me or my family, I wondered. Or both? What explained these patterns, and how could I change them? It was a question I'd only learned to ask about myself because of Jill.

While Jill and I were at Carnegie Mellon University, she studied conceptual art: the art of working with ideas. A project she did in 1992 explored truth in relationships. She realized not lying was not the same as being honest. Truth in a relationship was something you had to actively pursue. It didn't happen on its own. For the project, she picked ten people she was closest to and wrote them honest letters about her relationship with them. I remember thinking it was a crazy idea, and I rejected it immediately. But then I realized my rejection was based entirely on how terrified I'd be to do it myself. Who was entirely honest with anyone, much less their parents, siblings, and closest friends?

The more Jill explained about the project, the more impressive it seemed. It was a simple way to explore the most important questions we have: Who are we close with? What does it mean to be close? How intimate is any relationship where we're afraid to write an honest letter? I was studying philosophy at college, and her project explored many questions about identity in ways even philosophers, given their safe faith in abstraction, would be afraid to try. The project forced a comparison between imagined intimacy and reality. Would your best friend be angered by what you have to say, or take the letter, as challenging as it might be to read, as a gift, an invitation to respond and share in kind? I didn't think I was brave enough to do it myself. But Jill wrote one of her ten letters to me, and I wrote back. A few years later we got married, and we're still together today.

I thought about Jill's project often as I grew into my late twenties. It was a major inspiration for how many times I reached out to my father and my family to try and improve our relationships. I'd been a lousy friend, never returning phone calls to my oldest and best ones, and I worked on those bad habits. I sorted out much of my past with my brother, mother, and even Tracy, but the mystery of my father remained. There was something dark and scary between us that I'd ignored, but it grew bigger and demanded more attention with each passing year.

I developed an obsession with songs about fathers and sons. Many early Bruce Springsteen songs are heavy with lyrics about battles with Douglas Springsteen, his father. Douglas was a quiet, sad man who, like George Lucas' father, never supported Bruce's dreams. Springsteen's songs expressed feelings I felt but didn't have words for, feelings I thought I was alone in the world for having. One song, "My Father's House," is about a man waking up from a dream, a dream of being afraid in the darkness. He flees in the dream for the safety of his father and then wakes up trembling. He soon finds himself thinking about why he was so distant from his father and drives to his house to reconcile. It's a song of a deep longing to fix the past.

I listened to that song dozens of times. I learned to play it on guitar so I could sing it myself. I knew I needed to make that drive. I'd been waiting my whole life for my father to come to me, but that was never going to happen. I was an adult, I realized. If I wanted something to happen, I had to lead the way. But in the oldest, deepest parts of myself, I didn't want to do it. It would bring up the past and stir up feelings I had buried and hidden for my entire life, emotions I didn't want to experience again. I didn't know what I would find or who I would be, but the idea wouldn't leave me alone. I'd stay awake at night running through old memories and playing out arguments in my mind.

Art Alexakis' father abandoned him and his mother when he was ten years old. He wrote an angry song called "Father of Mine" about how, as an adult, he looks back on his father's choices. Unlike Springsteen, Alexakis expressed no interest in reconciliation. It's a one-way message to a man who probably never heard the song. There's none of the longing that Springsteen expresses. There's an uncomfortable hostility in "Father of Mine" that I resonated with. The song gave me words that matched how I often felt. But for me, there was something beyond the anger. I loved my father. I wanted his attention and his love. What I most needed to do was tell him of my disappointment, not to wound him or get revenge, but to see if we could get past those differences and do something better with the time we had left. I wanted to know who my father was, now, in the present. Finding the courage to try and know my father would also help me discover who I was now, as an adult.

The song "My Father's House" ends sadly. The narrator, after his dark dream, takes the long drive to where his father lives. When he arrives and knocks on the door, a stranger answers. She says only that whoever he's looking for doesn't live there anymore. The song ends with a line about how his father's house still calls to him, despite what he knows about it now. It's a song about the failure of longing. You can't fix the past, no matter how many times you try to go back. If you spend your life trying to fix it, you become a slave to history and make new mistakes in the present for it. The ambition must be to use the past to help with the present.

Bruce Springsteen was lucky. Years after he wrote those songs, his father had a stroke, and miraculously, his personality changed for the better. He discovered access to his warmer emotions and shared them openly with Bruce. Their relationship improved, giving Bruce many of the things he'd always wanted and needed. It was an unexpected and unlikely turn of events and one I hoped for myself. I thought initiating the conversation with my father, now as an adult, could be the beginning of something like that for us. I could talk to him as a man, and as two men, we could work together to be friends. But to get there, I had to escape the past.

When I knew I'd be visiting home in May of 2000, I promised myself this was it. I was twenty-eight years old. I was happily married. I owned a house and was fully grown in many ways. I didn't want to spend any more time imagining myself confronting my father; I wanted to do it so I could move on, regardless of what the outcome would be. Like Todd throwing me into the deep water, thinking about this was worse than doing it, and I'd already spent hundreds of hours thinking.

Jill gave me advice on where to start. She suggested I speak from my feelings. This was great advice, as I'd imagined bullying him into submission, as arguing was generally my way. I'd imagined handing him a litany of grievances and complaints that, through precise arguments, would use the crowbar of logic to win my case. I had a crude efficiency in relationships at the time, believing the most direct path to the point was the best. Of course, I had few examples where this worked out well, but like my father, I was stubborn in my beliefs. I was lucky to have Jill's advice and wise enough to use it.

I wrote long entries in my journal. I even wrote a detailed letter to my father, never intending to send it, but purely to help me think and feel things through. Is this really what I've been feeling? Is this how I'd explain it? What was at the core underneath the stories and memories I'd considered for so long? I felt such deep anger at him, but the more I worked, the more I realized how convenient anger was. Anger was never the source. I didn't just get angry; I got angry because I was hurt.

What was it at the core of all the slights, wounds, and disappointments that hurt me?

Finally I realized what it was. I never felt important to him. I never felt I was worth his time or attention. I felt, for much of my life, unworthy. And the more I let my feelings around worth linger over me, the more I realized this was at the heart of everything. This was the way to start the conversation. The only questions left were when I would bring it up and if I'd have the courage when it counted. I discovered how much scarier it would be to speak honestly to my father than anything I'd done before. Debate and argument was easy, as it was nothing more than rhetoric and abstractions. To simply say, "I feel hurt," or "I feel unworthy" was terrifying by comparison.

Early in the evening on May 25, 2000, I decided tonight was the night. I'd arrived from Seattle the night before and wanted relief from the pressure of carrying this burden. We ate dinner that night at the same table I'd eaten meals at my entire childhood. My mom made chicken cutlets, mashed potatoes, and green peas, one of my favorite meals as a child. The meal had the usual positive joy we shared in the early days of any of my visits. But I remember staring at my father for a long moment while he talked to my mother. I wondered about what I was going to say and what was going to happen. Had he any idea this day would ever come?

We moved to the living room, a place I'd sat in thousands of times to watch TV or play Atari video games with Todd. We talked for another hour, but I barely paid attention, my mind preoccupied. Mom, as usual, was the first to go to bed. When she mentioned feeling tired and leaving soon, my heart picked up its pace. I felt a buzz in my hands and fingertips. My body knew what was about to happen and was getting ready. Throughout the night, I'd rehearsed my opening line to my father in my mind. I didn't want to chicken out but was afraid that I would. I knew my best odds were doing it right away rather than waiting for a perfect moment that would never come. My mother said goodnight, walked down the hall, and closed the bedroom door. My father and I were all alone.

Sitting across from him, as I'd been all night, I said, "Dad, I have something I need to talk to you about." I looked into his eyes, eyes I'd feared for as long as I could remember. Was I a child or a man now, I wondered. I was twenty-eight years old, but looking at him now, I still felt like a child. I vibrated between one and the other, trying to hold on to the fact that I was both. I was his son, but I was now coming to him as a man. And to think of myself as a man for the rest of my life, I had to go through with what I'd planned.

He answered more with a nod than with words: "Okay, sure. What is it?"

I told him my opening line. "Dad, I don't feel important to you."

And he listened. He asked, "What do you mean?" without malice, but with curiosity.

And I explained what I'd been feeling and for how long. "For most of my life, I've never felt important to you. It always seemed like your time went to other things besides me."

He had questions, but he didn't get upset. He wasn't warm in the way my mother would be in the same conversation. He wasn't understanding or empathetic, but he was calm. I was greatly relieved by this. I'd expected worse. I'd imagined a hundred different ways it would devolve into yelling and screaming and someone, possibly me, storming out of the house forever. We talked quietly for a half hour. He decided he wanted to go to bed, but offered that we should talk about this again. When he left and closed the bedroom door behind him, something in me shifted – like a foundation of a building that had been off-center finally sliding toward its rightful place.

After I returned home to Seattle, we talked on the phone every few weeks. These were hard, slow conversations. Without Mom around, he was hard to talk to. He didn't say much. He struggled with the basics of finding topics to talk about, doing his best when the conversation was about him. But to his credit, he showed up on the other end every time and gave it his best. He listened to my thoughts on the past, which put him in a bad light. Occasionally he'd concede a point about what he should have done differently with me when I was young. Soon he proposed we take a trip together to Yellowstone National Park. It was likely an idea my mother suggested, but he deserves credit for making the offer. We set a date for July to meet in Wyoming, the first trip we'd taken alone together since those childhood outings during my parents' separation twenty years before.

One major mystery I wanted to solve was why my father had the first affair – the only one at the time. It caused so much suffering, yet I'd never heard him explain why he did it. What did he think the outcome of the affair was going to be? I met his first mistress once, Cathy, when he took me to lunch with her one summer day. She was nice to me in the same way my mother's boyfriends were to me at the time. I wanted to know who my father was then, now that I was about the age he was during that time. There were many questions inside our family that no one had discussed, ever, and if I had unresolved feelings about it, I'm sure Tracy, Todd, and perhaps Mom did too. He'd had decades to think about it, and now I wanted his answers. If he couldn't explain it now, he probably never would.

My distance from my father was part of a larger feeling: the sense that I didn't belong in my family. I didn't fit. I was too curious and confident, a poor match for the dominant personalities in our home. I'd never said this out loud, but it explained why all through high school I was compelled to get away. I wanted to go to a place where I felt I belonged.

Around the same time as our trip to Yellowstone, I took a trip alone with Mom for similar reasons. Although my relationship with her had always been good, I'd had a shortage of time alone with her too. We took a cruise to Glacier Bay in Alaska and one day went out into the water on a two-person kayak. It was quiet and beautiful, a perfect moment to talk about things we wouldn't often discuss. She sat in the seat in front of me as we paddled around the bend from the cruise ship, alone together in the wilderness. When we stopped paddling, we could hear the most beautiful kind of silence, only the wind over the water and the trees in the distance swaying gently on the shores.

She asked me about the past, and I told her I had something I'd figured out recently. I said, "Mom, I hope you don't take this the wrong way, but I've never felt like I fit into our family."

"Really?" she said.

And I replied, "Yeah, I always felt close to you and Todd, but somehow that wasn't enough. I was always at odds with the family as a whole, fighting to feel like myself. And that's why I was in such a rush to leave. I felt that to be myself I had to be somewhere else."

In the kayak, I couldn't see my mother's face, only the back of her life jacket. It made conversation seem otherworldly, as if I wasn't speaking through sound, but through telepathy instead. It made it easier in a way, as both of us could look into the peaceful distance as we talked.

To my surprise, she understood completely. She was almost enthusiastic about it. It was so strange to have a realization of mine, the crystallization of an abstract feeling I'd carried for most of my life, to be acknowledged by my mother. She shared that she'd never felt like she belonged in her family as a child either. It was only later, as an adult, that she reconciled with her brothers and sister and formed better bonds.

What bothered me later that night, as I tried to sleep in the tiny cruise ship cabin we shared, was why she didn't take it as a failure on her and Howard's part that I felt so alone. My mother slept well, but I found the confined space unnerving on that trip, and often, in search of relief, looked out the small port window of our cabin. I remember that night looking to the sea, under the gentle moonlight, and seeing something swimming along with the boat. I watched carefully until I saw it stop and crest above the water. It was a young seal. I could clearly see its two round, curious eyes, watching my mother, my world, and me float on by, without a care in the world for who its parents were or who it was supposed to be.

My youthful isolation took many forms, but the strongest was basketball. During my parents' separation, and forever after, basketball was my sanctuary. I was my most confident self on the court, whether practicing alone or playing against strangers. My brother used to drive me to the Samuel Field Y on Saturdays, and we'd play until they kicked us out at the end of the night. Basketball helped me connect with people and find myself, and still does today. In movies, families rally around child athletes, helping them prepare for the big game or taking their son or daughter out for dinner to celebrate victories. We were not that kind of family.

Basketball was my dream. It was the one thing I worked harder at than anything. But no one at home noticed how hard I worked. There was also little recognition of my successes. When I made the varsity team my junior year, it was a tremendous triumph, the greatest achievement of my entire life. I was the first person in our family to play a varsity sport, something I was immensely proud of. But there was no one to celebrate it with. It had no meaning in that house. And as my pride in basketball grew, my distance from my family grew with it.

I've only had one encounter with my father about basketball, and it was when I was eighteen. It was the summer of 1990, just before I left for college. I trained every day, hoping to be good enough to make it as a walk-on player for their team, to keep my dream alive. One Saturday, I was training in the backyard, doing agility drills, jumping over ropes and sprinting across the small court, my shirt heavy with sweat from how hard I was working. My father, who I hadn't seen in the backyard since I was a child, came outside. He asked if he could join me. He must have seen me from his bedroom window and for some reason, today, decided to reach out to me. I didn't know what to say, as this had never happened before. It was the first time in my life he stood on a basketball court with me. I offered him the ball.

He took the ball and dribbled it awkwardly. Then he shot at the hoop, shooting the ball from his shoulder, not gently as I tried to do, but as if it had the weight of a bowling ball. I stepped forward to try and show him, but he was in his own world, catching the rebound himself and shooting again. I didn't know what to do with the fact that he didn't know what to do. He was unaware that I was training and that for me this place was special, as close to a church as I'd ever have. I just watched, frozen between worlds. I know I didn't make him feel welcome. I was scared and awkward, afraid he'd make a joke at my expense – perhaps something about the pointlessness of basketball and why it was a lesser sport, the things he'd say when I watched the NBA on TV in the living room. What did he want from me here? I didn't know. A few minutes later, he left, and I was relieved.

I see now it was an echo of our encounter at the front door during the separation. Back then I was just eight years old, fumbling with that screen door. This time it was him fumbling with a basketball. He was always on one side, and I on the other, both looking for something we didn't know how to get. On the basketball court, I was a decade older than I was the day at the door. At eighteen years old, I understood enough to hope, somewhere in the deepest parts of my mind, that he'd come back to the court. If he came a second time or a third, it would have been less strange. There would have been room to figure it out. Maybe he'd offer, or I'd ask him, to help me train, which I desperately needed. But I never saw him with a basketball in his hands again. This trip to Yellowstone was nearly a decade since that day on the basketball court. Now as adults, it was a third chance for us to stand alone together, and I wanted more than anything for this to be the one that turned things around.

Yellowstone is one of the largest calderas in the world. A caldera is a super volcano. The reason there are amazing geological sites throughout this national park is because of what's been happening underground for thousands of years. The last eruption of this volcano was 600,000 years ago, and the destruction was large enough to cover half the continent with ash and debris. I considered this as I walked around the sites with my father. It's one of the most beautiful places in the world, yet the beauty is born from the power of destruction. Much like the reasons my father and I were there, it was beautiful and dangerous at the same time.

When we checked into our little wood cabin, a single room with two old beds, there was nothing on the walls. There was no television, radio, or telephone, only a simple, gray light fixture hanging from the ceiling, with a string to turn the light on and off. My father and I would have few distractions from each other. When he arrived in the room, I watched him stand over his bed, looking down, mystified by his own luggage. He looked back and forth between the duffle bag, sitting open on his bed, and a little piece of paper in his hand. He seemed irritated by this, and I didn't understand what was going on. Then I realized it was a map of his bag my mother had made for him. She'd made this map because she'd packed his clothes.

As we drove through the park, I'd learn the mechanics of how the caldera created the wonders of Yellowstone. The Old Faithful Geyser is heated by the same thermals that will blow the fifty-mile-wide plateau into the sky someday. The amazing prismatic pools, parking-lot-sized bodies of water in rainbow colors, so large and breathtaking they take a half hour to walk around, exist only because of bacteria that live in the high temperatures of the water there. The strange kinds of beauty I discovered compelled me to ask questions about how these things were made. The answer was always time. If you had the patience of time, the world made beautiful things to see all on its own.

At night we'd go out for dinner and have our serious conversations. We'd walk the hundred yards down the hill to a beautiful lodge, with wide wooden tables and a car-sized fireplace in the center, an endless supply of logs to fuel it in a stack at its feet. During these fireside chats, it was hard to ignore that we fit an unexpected cliché. There were many fathers, sons, brothers, sisters, and families around us. I'd see them at meals and think to myself that I knew their story, how they were reconnecting to keep the bonds of the past alive. We must have looked like them even though our mission was the opposite. We were trying to create bonds out of a past that didn't have many.

One night at the Old Roosevelt Lodge, the fanciest restaurant we could find near our cabin, we had our most intense conversation. He asked me what I found wanting about him as a parent. I wasn't sure I should answer at first. It seemed like a question he should answer on his own or with friends, his brother, or someone who could comment as a peer, not as his child. But I knew he had no one like this in his life. And here I was, wanting to tell him what I thought, wanting to relieve myself of this judgment I'd carried my whole life.

I spoke of his absence, echoing the statement that got us there: the feeling of unworthiness. He asked for evidence, not aggressively, but from a place of ignorance. He really seemed to have no idea what I was talking about or what could have created this void I felt. I talked about teaching myself to shave. How my mother signed all my report cards. How he taught me nothing about friendships or girls or how to be a man. I mentioned how he offered no help with the thousands of hours I spent chasing my dream of playing basketball. I wasn't mean or angry, but there was a weight to my words I know he felt. He asked questions about these stories, and I answered them, and then he asked more. But he didn't like where it led. Eventually he smiled the kind of smile he'd given me my whole life: a smile that he was proud of, as if he'd figured something all out in his mind and was waiting to share to enhance his pleasure.

He laughed slightly and then looked me straight in the eyes. Still smiling, he said: "Your problem is you remember too much."

Sitting there in that restaurant at Yellowstone, I looked down in despair at the half-eaten meal on my plate. There had been so much hope in me for this trip, for my father and for my life, and those words stripped those hopes away. I wasn't hungry anymore, for my meal or for love from him. He was still my father. His words felt final, even if in my mind I knew they were absurd. What he said had precisely the desired effect of leaving me speechless and alone. He won that round in the same way he always did, using rhetoric that guaranteed, in the long run, he'd lose me again. My father was time traveling again, retreating to the past when he didn't like the present, and insisting on the present when he didn't like the past.

I do realize now, in a way, that my father was right. If he were a different kind of person, there is something to be said for starting over. But that can only have a chance of success if something has been learned from what has already happened. Where do two people's memories of their past match? Where do they differ? In what ways? What feelings are shared, and which ones are surprises? It's only in discussing the past that we can find private truths and make them shared ones. There are gems in the dirt of every relationship if we're willing to dig to find them.

We left Yellowstone agreeing to talk on the phone every few weeks, and he lived up to that promise. But the night before each phone call, I never slept well. My mind raced through the things I imagined he'd say, and I'd practice in my mind how to respond. I read books on fathers and sons. I talked to Jill and Todd often, asking for advice. I didn't want to obsess about these phone calls, but not wanting to obsess only made the obsession stronger. Every movie or news story about a father and son I came across I felt personally. I'd put myself and my father in those stories, comparing and evaluating, feeling sad or lost. I was constantly reminded of this old wound, now exposed to myself and the world. Yellowstone made it impossible to pretend it wasn't there anymore. A life-time of feelings I'd been hiding away were now coming out.

When we spoke, the conversations fell into familiar patterns. I'd reference some of the conversations we had at Yellowstone, but with new questions and ideas. He didn't remember them. He said he was surprised I didn't feel important to him when I was a child. He asked again for stories of the past, questioning me on why I thought he didn't come to my basketball games, hinting at his lack of memory about any of it at all. I was confused at first. How could he not remember? I'd walk him through it all again, and eventually he'd come around and acknowledge that what I told him was true. But weeks later, when we spoke again, we'd play the same game. It would take an hour or more to get him back to the same place I'd worked so hard to get to in the last call. There was a message here for me I wasn't getting. He was on the phone, but he wasn't really there.

But I was relentless. I asked him to read John Bradshaw's *Bradshaw On: The Family*, the only book I knew of then about family dynamics. He refused, saying he read the first chapter, and, "I already know everything the book is going to say." I wrote him emails. I asked who his role model as a father was, or is, and he said he didn't have one. I suggested he consider this question, not for the past, but for now, but he expressed no interest. Phone call after phone call I slowly realized what he was trying to tell me. Perhaps he had no capacity for doing anything more than showing up. I thought of his father, my grandfather, sitting on that orange couch staring in silence at the TV. My grandfather had been in the same room, but not the same world; perhaps my father was just the same way.

In the summer of 2003, I visited my parents' new house in Connecticut, and he and I fell into a familiar argument about the past. It went too far, further than usual, with us yelling at each other from across the kitchen. My mother stormed in, screaming at us both. She was furious, but not about this fight; she was enraged about all of them. She said, with tears in her eyes, "The two of you need to stop and figure out how to get along! I'm so sick of this! Can you stop? Find a way to stop this, please!" She told us how she loved us both and didn't comprehend why we'd been stuck in the same place for so long. And then she walked off, leaving us, deflated, on our own.

My father and I, hours later, talked alone in the kitchen. I told him relationships require work. It was going to take effort to improve things. And he said, without much of a thought, perhaps the most honest thing he's ever said to me: "Why should I have to do any work? Can't we just talk about sports and simple things?"

He wasn't joking, as much as I wanted it to be a joke. He sincerely believed the answer, after all this, was to treat each other like acquaintances. To my surprise, it didn't make me mad. I'd had enough after months of working and working and getting nowhere. I'd finally exhausted myself, and hearing him say those words made me certain of it. I told him, "You don't have to do any work if you don't want to." And he smiled. And we both moved on. I went home the next day and never brought up improving our relationship again, and neither did he.

The thing I'd wanted, to know who my father was, had happened. He was, in the end, a strange man. The way he related to me was no worse than the way he related to everyone he'd ever known. He never wanted to do the work demanded by any of his relationships, but he liked to think that he did. He never wanted to be a parent, but he thought he did. He wasn't just a mystery to me; he was a mystery to himself. I found relief in this. Our relationship was fated to end here from the day I was born. It didn't matter what I did or who I was, as it had never been about me at all. Parents are just people. The limitations they have aren't put there by their children. I didn't choose him to be my father, but now, if I was strong enough, I could choose what I wanted to do about it.

I decided I had to see Howard as my mother's husband, a man in my life, but not in my life because of me. I cried over this. It was a deep cry, something I'd held on to for most of my life. It was the end of the deepest dream of my childhood, a dream I had before I knew what dreams were. I'd wanted a man in my life who would look out for me, help me get ahead in life, and put me before other things. I'd wanted a man who would be my ally, someone I could trust to be there for me. But when I accepted him for who he was and separated him from the dreams I'd had, the pressure I'd felt all my life began to fade away.

Todd taught me a lesson during those years after Yellowstone that helped tremendously. My visits to my parents did get easier and easier, but I'd find, once a visit, I'd end up in one of the old arguments with Howard, the same arguments we'd have at the dinner table in Queens. Todd asked: "Why do you always take Howard's bait?" I asked him what he meant, and he explained our father often made outrageous comments, words chosen specifically to get a rise out of me, or anyone, and start the debate. Of everyone in our family, I was the biggest sucker. Even after Yellowstone and all I'd learned, I still suffered from the legacy of wanting his acknowledgment and of wanting to prove him wrong. It was one of the oldest habits I had, but now, with all I'd learned, I knew I didn't need that acknowledgment anymore. I hadn't needed it for a long time.

On my next visit to my parents' house, with my brother's advice in mind, I waited for it to happen. One night, after dinner, we were all sitting at the dinner table. As we talked about the news together, my father soon said something outrageous, even for him. He said that a return to McCarthyism, and the blacklists he made for those suspected of betraying their country, was what this country needed today. I didn't argue. I didn't debate. Instead, I calmly told him how ridiculous a thing this was to say. I was able to do it without getting upset, because I didn't see him as my father anymore. He was just this man who had been in my life for a long time. He immediately called me closed-minded, and as personal attacks are a good sign of someone losing an argument, it was easy to walk away. I calmly said that what he'd said was offensive and he should apologize. And to my surprise, he did. My mother was even brave enough to lecture him about stooping so low, which I'm sure she had done in the past and would do again.

It was over these years, the time between my visit to Yellowstone in 2000 and the news of my father's second affair in 2012, that was the best time for my relationship with my father. Visits to my parents were easier. My father and I rarely argued. He'd instinctively put out his intellectual traps, but I rarely went for them anymore.

He'd often sit in silence at dinners when, without me leading the charge, no one took what he was offering. Dangling those seeds of arguments in front of his family was the only way he knew how to have a deep conversation, and when it stopped working, he became a smaller man.

Instead, I looked for territory he took comfort in and that also interested me. I'd arrive in Connecticut with lists of questions about his childhood, helping me understand the larger story of our family and what his parents were like. He enjoyed talking about himself, even if they were unpleasant subjects. I'd ask him, and my mother, about relatives who died before I was born. I learned how my great-grandfather David Berkun fled to the U.S. from Ukraine in 1902, running from conscription into what would become the Russo-Japanese war. I heard how David's brothers were killed in Europe during the rise of Germany decades later. Had David stayed in Europe, I would never have been born. I realized that, even as a nonreligious family, it was our Jewish heritage that explained the good parts of our dinner table debates, a practice so deeply embedded in our culture, we practiced it without knowing where it was from. Without a nation of their own, Jews adopted books and literacy as the primary way to stay connected, and debate was a way to keep those religious texts alive and in the culture. As the years went by, I didn't mind anymore that my father was a limited man, a person who felt most comfortable sharing only when Mom was around.

The one thing I took away from him was Father's Day. I'd always sent my mother and father cards or made phone calls on their special days. But with my eyes fully open to what kind of father mine turned out to be, I couldn't do it for him anymore. I'd send him something for his birthday, for him as a person, but on Father's Day, I'd be silent. Until he was willing to do the work of a father, I couldn't lie to him or myself about the role he played in my life. My only regret is not telling him why I stopped honoring his fatherhood. It shouldn't have been hard for him to guess, but I should have explained and left no doubts.

For years, I had peace. The anger I'd carried with me all my life was gone. I didn't linger in the past, even when I came to visit. It didn't bother me anymore to see stories about fathers and sons, and I noticed them less often. I was proud of the work I'd done on myself and with him, the hard kind of work few people do. I talked to Todd and Tracy about it all, and they told me my discoveries helped them, even if only in small ways. I no longer expected much from Howard, and that freed me to have fun and enjoy what we did share. I felt I was done with the past.

But here in this book you know more than I did then. I didn't know life can be a spiral, forcing me to face my issues again and again. I didn't realize that just because you're done with the past doesn't mean the past is done with you.

FOUR

....

LEGACY

The Old Testament says nothing about what Adam thought of Cain, or Cain of Adam. Adam and Eve are silent when Cain kills their younger son Abel. The only pain we hear is from the voice of God. But of course, it's God's unexplained rejection of Cain's offering of fruit that angers Cain in the first place. Silence is the evil in those passages. It's what's unsaid that leads to suffering. The feelings that must have been in everyone's hearts are never spoken or recorded. If Cain knew other means to express his anger, perhaps he'd have talked to his father figures, God or Adam, instead of expressing himself through violence. Some interpretations of Genesis extend God's curse of Cain to his offspring, making future generations pay the price for what Cain did.

We are all like Cain, and his children, in a way. Springsteen wrote a song called "Adam Raised a Cain" that asks questions of unavoidable legacy. "You inherit the sins, you inherit the flames" is a line from the song that, despite how many times I'd heard it, I'd never applied to my life until this past year. As much as I hated my father's ways, it was impossible not to be like him. No matter how I try to be more open, more self-aware, more joyous about life, I will always only have one father. The sound of my laugh, the proportions of my hands, and the sharpness of my eyes all come from him, aspects of myself I can't escape. I can compensate, I can grow, I can learn, but at the end of it all, I still resemble him. No matter how much therapy I do or tough choices I make, deep inside me are elements of my father that I don't notice anymore, and realizing that scared me. I knew I wasn't like him in many ways, but what a convenient thing this was to believe.

I decided thinking about these things, which I did often, changed little. It was my habits for how I handled my feelings that needed work. I worked with a therapist and discovered the power of being honest with a stranger, a person who'd advised many other strangers about their inner lives. I recognized how many other father figures I'd had in my life that helped me and that I'd never told them the difference they made.

I started of course with my brother Todd, thanking him for how many things he'd done that shaped who I became. I wrote to Rob Elkins, my basketball coach at the Samuel Field Y. I found Adam Smith, one of my favorite summer camp counselors, on Facebook. I contacted Alan Stein, my high school history teacher, who showed me a more honest way to debate than the one

I'd learned from my father. I contacted Menachem Bazian, my Hebrew tutor, who gave me one of the best pep talks of my young life on the day of my Bar Mitzvah. There were so many circles that had been opened for me by men other than my father, circles that helped me, and I needed to close them. I thought it'd be wrong if these men never learned of the profound effect they'd had simply because I was too lazy to tell them.

I realized, as I approached the age of thirty, that I was a man now. I could choose to do with my time what all of those adults had done for me. I was the youngest in my family and had never had the chance to help a younger sibling. It was obvious I should volunteer to be a big brother at Big Brothers Big Sisters. My own big brother had done so much to help me, but he was just a child too during those early years. An adult who was interested in me, or any child in a situation like mine, could have done so much more.

That year, through Big Brothers Big Sisters, I met Derek, a young teenager whose father lived many miles away. We'd go out together each week, often to watch the local high school football games. Sometimes I'd watch him play on his little league baseball team. I was surprised at how easy our relationship was. We both genuinely wanted to do things together. Much like me, he just needed someone older, someone safe and friendly, to share time with. He's twenty-four now and doing well, and we're still friends to this day.

Spending time with Derek, the activities we'd schedule and plan, often made me think of when I'd see my father late at night. I often went several weekdays in a row without seeing him, as I'd go to bed before he came home. But when I was a senior in high school, with no real curfew anymore, I was often the only one awake at 11:30 p.m., watching TV before I went to bed. It happened to be the same time my father sometimes arrived home from work or the racetrack.

From the couch, I'd hear the hum of the garage door opening, and I'd know he was almost home. In every one of those moments, I faced the same question: Do I go to bed before he gets inside, or do I stay here in the living room and talk to him? Sometimes I'd carefully look down from the window and watch his car, with his yellow turn signal blinking in the night, turn off the street and up our driveway. In those brief moments, I'd look down in silent thought, debating my options.

Sometimes I felt I should stay. I liked being around him when he was in a good mood. He was working to provide for us, and someone should welcome him home. On some nights, I knew Johnny Carson had a guest, Magic Johnson or George Carlin, that I wanted to see. But just as often, I went to bed. I was tired myself, and it was hard to start a conversation with anyone so late. And on those nights, I went to my room and hid, not out of fear of him, but out of something else: out of fear for the way I felt around him. It was the bottom of the barrel of his day, and to stay would be to accept the last scraps not spent on strangers at the racetrack. I had too much pride to participate. Unlike what I'd learn from my training at Big Brothers Big Sisters, there was no promise made by an adult for a specific window of time to share, something all children deserve. But since these late night encounters were all that I had, the nightly debate ensued: do I stay, or do I go?

When I did stay, he'd ask me about my day. I'd answer briefly, knowing he didn't know my friends' names and didn't care about basketball, the two important things in my life. He'd be charming if he'd done well with the horses that night, but more often he'd talk about how close he came. We'd sit at the kitchen table, taking the Entenmann's chocolate doughnuts out of the freezer and finishing half the box with tall glasses of milk. He'd always take a tiny piece of a doughnut out of the box, barely a quarter of it, saying that was all he wanted. Just a taste, he'd say. But then as we talked, he'd take another piece away and another until, to his surprise, there was nothing left of the doughnut at all.

By January of 2013, my emails to my father remained unanswered. His last email to me was from November 14 of 2012, a reply to the email I'd sent at Mom's request, welcoming him home to Connecticut from Australia. There had been no phone calls. No holiday greetings. Nothing. I continued to talk to my mother and brother, and heard updates about him through them. There wasn't much to say. He had yet to decide about his future, and my mother was willing to let him return to their home in the hopes of convincing him to stay.

I was glad not to hear from him. It was consistent, something I had longed for throughout the months of confusion our family had been through. I felt increasingly like he wasn't a part of my family, regardless of whether he thought I was in his. But I didn't want to be like him. I didn't want to just disappear. Or perhaps, even if I'd never have admitted it, I still had the same fantasy my mother did: that he was capable of more than he'd shown before.

On 1/5/13, 12:46 PM, "Scott Berkun" wrote:

I've been doing my absolute best to try and reach out to you during this confusing and difficult time. I still understand very little and you haven't offered much about what you've done, what you're doing now, and what it means for you, our family, and for me.

The most generous interpretation I've found is this: you're confused and uncertain and need time to figure things out, but that's a guess. You haven't said much. From August through November you didn't respond to my emails at all, which perhaps you have some explanation for, but I don't know what it is.

I'd like to have some kind of relationship with you. For that to work you need to meet me half way, which has not been happening.

If you're not ready for that, that's ok - provided you make
that clear.

Love,

-Scott

A few days later, he had a one-line reply.

On 1/8/13, 8:53 AM, "Howard Berkun" wrote:
> Yes, this is correct.

It was a joke. It made me laugh to read it. That's all I
get? After all this, it's one sentence. But I know now I
have myself to blame. I was keeping in touch. I was
reaching out. I was giving him the benefit of so many
valid doubts, and he was giving me the benefit of nothing. I'd written him a letter with a way out already inside, and perhaps that's what I wanted: a way to let the
game go on without me ending it. Maybe I didn't want
him to win by being able to say I'd given up on him. But
I was done here. I promised myself I wouldn't reach out
again. It turned out a few weeks later I wouldn't have to.
He reached out to me.

From: Howard
Date: Thursday, February 21, 2013 at 8:55 AM
To: Scott Berkun

Subject: visit

hi Scott,

We havent spoken in a while. With all that has been going on, this has been a side effect. I would like to come out to be with you for a few days. Spend a little time together and chat and all that. I think it would be good. If you have time this weekend, I would come out on Saturday and stay few days.

I've always been fascinated by his mastery of passive language. "We haven't spoken in a while" makes it sound like cloudy weather, something that happened all on its own, and we were just witnesses to it. It was nice to hear from him, but I couldn't help but notice the trigger on this offer: he wanted to visit in two days. It was doughnuts at night after he'd come home from the track. After all this time, what was the rush? There wasn't one. I took it to be another game: just barely enough effort that he could say he tried, yet so little effort that he knew I'd say no. I made no judgment of it. I suggested we start with a phone call, as we hadn't spoken in almost a year. He agreed to call me on Saturday, and with this, my anxiety returned. I couldn't keep my mind from playing the old games, the games I'd learned from Yellowstone, of trying to work out every argument in my head. I was angry with myself for it. I'd hoped I was better than this, but I wasn't.

When I answered the phone, he opened with a joke. He asked me how the Seattle Mariners were doing. It wasn't baseball season, and I wouldn't have known even if it was, as I've never followed baseball. It was his attempt to find comfort for himself masquerading as charm. But I didn't laugh, and he didn't like that I didn't laugh. He asked if this was a bad time, and I told him this was as nice as he was likely to find me on any day.

He immediately questioned my emails, asking why I'd been so critical of him over the last few months. I found this ridiculous and told him so. I told him he should be grateful he'd heard from me at all. He played his games for a few minutes. I heard Todd's voice in my mind, "Don't take the bait, Scott. Don't take the bait." And I didn't. When he failed to get a rise from me, he offered that my anger at him was because I was scared for Mom. I told him I thought she was an adult and could fend for herself. I said I would understand if he moved to Australia or got divorced or joined the circus. Whatever he thought he needed to do in his life, I'd support in a way, and this was true. I would be happy for him if any choice made him a happier person with what was left of his life. But I told him he needed to decide. He had dragged every relationship in his family through a nightmare. I wished him luck. I told him, "Dad, I hope you figure out how to be happy," and I meant it.

That my father was a narcissist was undeniable. He was, as I had to keep reminding myself, also a very strange man. He was genuinely mystified by what I said in our phone call, as if I were speaking about some alien species of animals. He'd probably been just as mystified at Yellowstone or with any of hundreds of moments of intimacy he's had with people in his life.

What I'd forgotten was the entire myth of Narcissus, the story the term comes from. In the myth, Narcissus sees an image of himself in the water but doesn't realize it's his reflection. He can't see himself. The reflection is beautiful to his eyes and reciprocates his every move, leading him to fall in love with what he sees. He spurns the one woman who truly cares for him, a nymph named Echo. In tears, she flees to the mountains. She becomes one with the stone, speaking only when others speak first. Narcissus, now alone with what he loves, reaches out to the image in the water. He despairs at how it disappears in the ripples that form when his finger touches it. He can't escape the horror of how the thing he loves abandons him. He slowly starves to death by the water, staring at his own image, not knowing who he is.

Two months after the phone call, it was my birthday. For all my life, my birthday presents came with cards signed, "From Mom and Dad," written in my mother's handwriting. I suspect many of them were as much a surprise to him as they were to me. Giving gifts just wasn't something fathers did, I often thought. He didn't much like receiving them either, and our family was never good at the practice, certainly not me and Todd. On this birthday, my forty-first, my father sent a present in an email.

There was only a brief message: "Happy birthday Scott. Birthday to 41." Below were five very old photographs, pictures of me and my father from years past. Since we'd spent so little time together, these must have been hard to find. These images of the two of us in the same physical space were so rare that most of them had been cropped from old photos. Some had to be magnified so far that they were heavily pixelated. The sight of them made me ill, not for the images themselves, but for their meaning. How could this be a gift? Why would I want to remember everything that was wrong with the past? He was in every photo, a haunting image to me now after everything he'd done that year. Our best times as father and son had been after Yellowstone, not before, but he'd forgotten. I was back in time again, invisible to him as a person with thoughts and feelings of my own.

I wrote this note, expecting to never hear from him again:

From: Scott Berkun
Date: Tuesday, April 16, 2013 at 6:37 PM
To: Howard
Subject: Re: Happy Birthday Scott

I'm sad for you. You're lost and you still don't realize how lost you are and how much damage you've done.
[...]

As far as these photos: they make me sad. I'm guessing you sent them in an attempt to remind me of happier times, but these were not happy times for me.

We talked at length at Yellowstone about how I felt about my childhood with you, but perhaps you've forgotten. You were not around much. When you were, you were often scary and distant. You spent more time at the track than you did helping me sort out my young life.

I am absolutely grateful you provided for me as a parent. You made sure I went to college. You paid for my clothes and needs. You entertained my arguments at the dinner table, and I learned how to think and reason, things that are critical parts of who I am. But the two of us rarely spent time alone together. And I grew up alone in that house. I trained for basketball alone. I figured out my friendships, girlfriends and myself, alone. There is a void where you should have been and you know that - you can't try to bank on those times now. It was a mistake to send me these photos. It was not a gift to see these things.

As far as you and I - you've spent your life depending on Judi to relate to your own children - now that you've betrayed her, you're on your own with me. You have no idea what you're doing. You are either brave or crazy to try. If you want to salvage your relationship with me, you have a lot of work to do, work you've hid from your whole life, as I don't think you understand relationships at all.

Over the last months I see you as a fool, a lost soul, or an asshole - I can't tell which anymore - maybe it's some of all.

I'd guess you think I'm saying all this to hurt you. But I'm not. I have no interest in hurting you. But I feel I owe you my honesty rather than responding with silence. And if you read this more than once you'll notice I've written it very carefully with that in mind.

I hope you figure yourself out and find happiness.
I hope you're seeing a therapist.
I hope you are honest with them.
I hope you're getting help.
I hope you're brave enough to share this email with them.
I do sincerely wish you well.

-Scott

In *The Return*, a Russian film directed by Andrey Zvyagintsev, two young boys are surprised to find their father is home. He disappeared mysteriously when they were infants, and now, years later, he is back. He is a strong, quiet man, and the first morning they are together, he takes them on a long drive, with their mother's silent permission. While they're both in awe of his powers, with strong shoulders and tough eyes, they're terrified of him too. During the trip, they do what he says out of respect for the idea of a father. They don't know him, but they know the concept of a father, and they use that instead. They respect him because they want to be the kind of sons that their father, whoever he is, will be proud of. But his return, and their journey together, is filled with more mysteries than answers.

I watched this powerful film intensely. It spoke to moments and feelings I'd never been able to explain to others. I asked my mother to watch it too, and she immediately compared the boys to me and Todd: how the oldest tried harder to follow along, while the youngest questioned everything, demanding answers his father didn't want to give. It's not a film of resolutions; instead, it's a film of questions, the kind of movie many people don't like. But I found part of myself in this movie. Some of the mysteries of my childhood were acknowledged. It possessed some of the secrets that I couldn't easily explain.

Art is how you find yourself. Somewhere out there is a poem or a song that can tell you something you need to hear or capture a fear you didn't know had a name. Listen carefully to your favorite songs, and pay attention in your favorite books, and you'll see artists desperately sorting through what they can't explain in their lives. When done well, art captures the essence into a song, a story, a book, or a poem that transforms you. It imbues those feelings into an object that lives on in the world, long after the artist is gone. The mere existence of that object is satisfying, at least to its maker, and hopefully to the consumer. It proves those feelings are worthy. Perhaps it makes it easier to escape the sadness of the past, not by solving problems, but by validating that they're real.

It should be no surprise my father never replied to my email, but there was other progress. My mother had been seeing a therapist and convinced my father to see one too. He invited Todd to come to a session, as like the older brother in *The Return*, he was a better place for my father to start. Sadly, it didn't last. He was never invited again. Todd had the same opinion I did at the time: Howard needed to decide. Even my Mom, after talking and talking about it for weeks, admitted to herself this had gone on long enough.

She pressured Howard to make up his mind. Each time she pressured him, he'd invent new excuses. He'd claim to have forgotten about agreeing to a deadline. He'd say he wasn't feeling well. It wasn't until the end of April that she told him he had to move out. I was proud of her, if for nothing else, for making a decision on her own instead of waiting for him to make it for her.

With their winter home in Florida unoccupied, the home they'd driven down from Connecticut together to buy, he decided to go there. For weeks, he lived alone in an empty house. I imagine pizza boxes and Chinese take-out cartons lined up along his kitchen counter, a half-empty six-pack of Heineken in the fridge. He didn't know how to cook and knew no one within a hundred or even a thousand miles. I can see him driving at night to catch races at Gulfstream Park, the nearest racetrack and casino a half hour away. He was still in touch with his mistress in Australia all this time, and I wonder what their conversations were like. Was she too pressuring him to decide? I would have been if I were her. Their one-year anniversary "together" had passed, and their future was just as uncertain as it had ever been. I can still find empathy for him. It's hard for anyone to be alone and far away from home, or so confused about where home is and who to share it with.

One day my father didn't feel well, and then another. He went to the doctor and explained he'd had to go to the bathroom more often than usual. Something was different. They ran some tests and called him the next day. It was cancer.

My father had always been afraid of being sick and of dying. My mother had warned him, early on in this saga, about what might happen if he left his family behind. "Who will look after you?" she'd pleaded. But he'd ignored her. And now here he was, alone in an empty house, facing what might be the end of his life. Desperate, he texted my mother. Soon he was on a flight back to Connecticut to talk to his regular doctors. He stayed at first in a hotel but then called his brother, a man he'd been estranged from for much of his life, and asked if he could stay. His brother said yes. My father didn't know what was next for him, but in the middle of everything else, had stumbled into a fight for his life.

When my mother called me to share all this news, I didn't know what to say. It was another shock that took time to digest. She, at first, felt conflicted too. Soon she realized she was in a position to be needed again. She'd email me and Todd with updates on his health every week, never stopping to think if we'd want to hear them or not. I told her I very much wanted to stay in touch with her, but not if the only subject was him. The emails slowed and stopped, and soon my mother let my father move back in.

When she told me her decision on the phone, I told her I understood. And I did. In a way, this was perfect for her. The hole he'd made this year would be filled, not completely, but enough. She'd have someone to take care of. She'd have a purpose. It made sense for my mother, but not for me, not for our family, and not for her grandchildren. Her daily life might return to what it was before, but everything else would be harder. She and I had shared the same side of this crisis. I was the first person she'd called. We'd rallied together as a mini-family: my mom, Todd, and me. And now she was bringing him back in, leaving me out again on my own.

In August of 2013, my father sent me this email, with no subject:

From: Howard
Date: Tuesday, August 6, 2013 7:11 AM
To: Scott Berkun

I am so very sorry that i have hurt you.
Love you very much
-Dad

I've only seen my father cry once. During a visit home from college, he and I were up late watching TV. Mom had gone to sleep an hour earlier, and we were flipping through channels. It was the anniversary of

Mickey Mantle's death, the legendary player for the New York Yankees. Mantle had been my father's favorite baseball player when he was young. He was my hero too, as I wore his number "7" every year in little league. I played centerfield and was left-handed, just like Mantle. He meant something to me, though I'd never seen him play live like my father had.

We stopped to watch a show about Mantle's life. They talked about his tremendous promise as a young player, the pride of the Yankees for many years, before alcohol and fame took him down. I sensed something in my father; his energy was different somehow, sitting just a foot away. I looked to see him weeping, his eyes set on the screen in front of us but red with tears behind his glasses. He cried softly, like a mature man cries, not hiding from the feelings, but not sharing them with me either. He was in his own universe in that moment, feeling something deep and old he didn't know how to explain. I said and did nothing, as surprised as I was by this. Given who he was and how vulnerable he seemed in that moment, I wanted to leave him alone, not for me, but to give him privacy with whatever it was he was experiencing. I must have been nineteen or twenty, but I'd never seen him cry before, and of all the times I'd expected it to happen, watching TV late at night wasn't it.

The show about Mantle was brief, just a few minutes long, and when it ended, my father spoke. He told me Mantle had meant something special to him in his life. That baseball for my father was how he formed his identity as a boy, and it was Mantle in those years who was his idol. What my father said was not an invitation for a conversation; it was a conclusion, as so much of what he'd say was. When he finished, he changed the channel on the television, and we never spoke of it again. Something about my father's apology email reminded me of that day. Two rare, unexpected moments of grace.

But my father's email, in the context of everything, confused me. Unlike watching Mantle's story on a quiet, random night, our family was in crisis. He'd been silent for so long on so many things, and this was all he had to say? I felt angry, sad, empathetic, and enraged at the same time. Emotions don't fit into simple categories when we're dealing with the toughest situations in life. When people ask us how we feel, the assumption is there's a single answer, one feeling. But we can be happy and sad at the same time. We can love and hate the same people. Emotions overlap and shift in ways our language doesn't express. It takes hours, days, or years to sort them out, if we can at all.

After another restless night, I found one notion, one sentence, that tied all my feelings together. I wrote a brief message that said the simplest and most honest thing I could:

From: Scott Berkun
Date: Thursday, August 8, 2013 at 4:39 PM
To: Howard
Subject: Re:

I don't believe you.

I was beyond long, nuanced letters. If his apology was sincere, he'd offer me another. Or he'd call. He'd do something more than this. I didn't believe he was sorry in the way normal people are sorry, but of course, it was clear to me he was not normal. I didn't believe that if I called him to talk about how I felt he'd listen for long. But he never replied. I'm sure he took what I said as an insult and was hurt by it, but it was true. The truth hurts sometimes. For him, being hurt is grounds to run away, which he did. It was another important message he'd never answer.

Todd often described being with our father as a choice between being treated like a sucker or a jerk. If you spoke up for yourself, he treated you like you were out of line. He'd attack you immediately for being disrespectful. But if you didn't speak up, and let him treat you how he wanted, you were a sucker. He'd take advantage and make you feel low. There was no middle ground, no place to comfortably stand while keeping your self-respect. To be close to him demanded being small.

My father's behavior became strange. He didn't reply to my email, but he did click the "like" button on the Facebook page for one of my books, *The Myths of Innovation*, which was published in 2007. There was no message from him, just the notification from Facebook that he'd clicked on it. Weeks later, he did the same on another one of my books. I found it so unnerving that I unfriended him on Facebook. I couldn't justify how we were in a relationship anymore.

I told Todd he was my family now – that Amy, his wife, Joshua and Jessica, his children, and my wife Jill were all that remained of our family. Our mother had put herself in a most difficult place, and it was hard to know how her choices would impact me and Todd. With no children of my own, my brother's kids were the closest I'd ever come to having my own. In our gallows humor way, Todd and I joked that perhaps the two of us were the only family there'd ever really been.

Something important I gained during this crisis was a closeness with my mother I'd never had before. I'd always been the most distant and most independent child, and much of that was by my own choosing. Moving away to Seattle gave me a distance from my family I desperately needed, but that had more to do with my father than my mother. This year, however sad it was, brought us closer together than we'd ever been. To feel the window of that connection closing made me sad. We'd always been honest with each other, and I had to share with her how I felt.

From: Scott Berkun
Date: Sunday, September 22, 2013 8:44 AM
To: Judi Berkun
Subject: Sad

Hi Mom:

I've been trying to find a way to express how I feel these last weeks. It's intense sadness. I barely hear from you anymore. The last time we spoke was when you told me you were taking Howard back in. Since then I've heard from you less and less and most of your emails are dominated by notes about his health, which is of little interest to me.

I've gone from being a primary supporter of yours, talking to you every week or two, to something far less significant in your life. Over the last year I think we were closer than we'd ever been and now that's over and I feel the loss. Nothing has changed on my end, but everything seems to have changed for you.

Howard's horrible behavior over the last two years has been devastating for me, the worst kind of abandonment of us all. And now I can't help but feel abandoned by you - since you're with him again and have far less interest in me. I know that with him back in your life there's no easy way for me to stay connected with you. And that makes me sad. It's an unavoidable consequence of taking him back.

The most tragic element is perhaps that this continues to be a replay in the worst way of what you and Howard did to our family 30 years ago and it makes me sick that I'm confronted again with trying to sort this out on my own. This is a mess you and Howard are making and it is costing me greatly and *the only sane choice I have is to distance myself from the whole thing.*

I've thought about this and I'm not sure I'm even asking you for anything. I don't know how our relationship is supposed to work, if at all, anymore. Our family is such a complete disaster in so many ways I can't conceive of how to maintain my own integrity while participating in it. In many ways I know Todd is the only family I have left. I love you and do wish you well but needed to share this with you.

-Scott

My email was heavy-handed, but that was how I felt at the time. She replied quickly, with a long and very thoughtful email. It was apologetic and sincere. I thanked her for it. We soon talked on the phone, and within just a few minutes, we understood each other. I wasn't angry. I understood what she was doing and why. I was just sad at the loss I felt, not just with her, but with everything. I felt frozen, much like I remember feeling as a child. I wanted the connection I'd felt before: part of a team, a project, a group of people who shared something important. But I couldn't accept the pain that I knew would come with trying to stay involved. There were too many twists in the fragile rope my parents had to offer me and Todd, if there would be an offer at all.

What I wanted most was stability. It wasn't to abandon my parents or wish they were further away, but simply not to have them on my mind so often. I almost didn't care how things resolved themselves as long as they did resolve, for someone. In that sense, my father getting sick, forcing him to return to my mother, was the best thing that could have happened. Without it, he'd have stayed on the fence the rest of his life, and she would have sat there with him, complaining perhaps, but not moving, leaving it up to me and Todd to wait with her or walk away. I was choosing to walk away.

I told Mom and Todd, after we had all learned of the second affair, that I was going to write a book about our family. They were supportive and let me interview them both about what they remembered. As I worked on the book, I realized something was missing. Most of what I knew of my father's recent choices came from Mom. If I wanted to tell this story, the thing it needed most were facts only he could share. I was in Boston again to promote a new book in November of 2013 and planned to take that same old drive to visit my brother and mother in Connecticut. I decided I'd email my father to see if he wanted to be interviewed. I told him that given I was the one writing the book, and given our history, I doubted he'd want to participate, but I would interview him if he was willing. To my surprise, he replied the same day saying he was eager to talk.

I was terrified to put myself back into the temptation of my life, to return to this distant, broken man that I'd been compelled to seek attention from. But I was excited too. This was another chance to prove to myself how far

I'd come. This was work for me now, the work of writing this book. I was using him to help me do something important, help he'd never given me before. Despite his failures in the past, he was the only person who could help in this way for this project. If I could interview him with my integrity intact, I'd take another step toward putting many ghosts to rest.

When the day came, I found myself sitting in the kitchen of my brother's house. I'd learned from my mother that my father's health was better. He'd had major surgery, but it went well, and if things continued, he'd be fine for some time. I'd written notes for the interview in my blue notebook while on the flight from Seattle, and I sat alone, reviewing them. Jessica, my niece, came over and asked me what I was doing. Todd and Amy came into the room, and I looked to them before I answered, not sure what I was supposed to say; Jessica, as smart as she was, was only eleven. Todd nodded and gave me a smile. I asked Jessica what she knew about her grandfather, and she told me she knew that her grandmother was angry with him for going away. I told her, "Yes, that's true. And I'm writing a book about what happened. I'm making a list of questions to ask your grandfather. Do you want to help?" And she said yes. Josh, my nephew, joined in too, sitting on my lap.

Josh was eight, roughly the same age I was when my father had his first affair. I couldn't help but think, looking at them, what I would have asked if I'd been given a chance like this. I showed them the questions I had so far and asked if they had any to add. I asked Todd and Amy too. To my surprise, Jessica had the best ones. Some were questions even I was afraid to ask, but hearing her say them out loud gave me a boost of confidence, and I wrote them down. When the list was finished, I got my things together and got in my car. And I sat there, unmoving, afraid to even turn on the radio.

Since the day my father said he'd do the interview, I'd been thinking about the drive from Todd's place to my parents' house. I knew exactly the song I was going to play, and I made sure I had it on my phone. It was "My Father's House," by Springsteen. There's one version of the song where he opens with a story of driving at night through his old neighborhood several times a week, not knowing why he is doing it. He sees a therapist who tells him he's trying to fix something in the past, something that was important and broken but lives only in his memory. And the therapist tells him that as much as he wants to, it can't be fixed. And then Springsteen plays the opening chords of the song. I put the song on, put the car in gear, and headed up the road to where my father lived.

As I drove, my mind wandered back to those drives through Brooklyn with my father, sitting in silence, my eyes staring out the window into the distance. I thought about how far I'd come from being that sad little boy. I was a man of my own now. I imagined myself as a boy, back in my father's car during the separation, opening the door at a stop light and just walking home. I didn't have to be there anymore. I didn't have to listen to whatever he would have said. I didn't have to spend time in any of those memories. And I didn't have to take this drive I was taking that day, but I was doing it not for the past, but for the kind of man I was now. I was braver than I ever thought I could be, and not because I wasn't afraid, but because a part of me, the oldest parts that would always awaken around my father, were terrified. But I was doing it anyway.

I sang the song as I drove. I thought of the hard things that had pulled us apart. I thought of their house, which happened, matching the lyrics, to be up on a hill. I knew the drive by heart yet found myself unsure at some of the turns. Finding my way, I pulled up around the curving street and saw the home my sister used to live in, the house next door to my parents. I drove up the driveway and stopped the car. I took a photo of myself. I wanted to know what I looked like on that day before I got out of the car.

I walked up the path toward the house and felt the quiet in the air. It was an early afternoon, and no one else on the street was outside. With my notebook in one hand, I rang the doorbell with the other. I knew my mother wouldn't be there; she'd agreed to go out until I finished. It would be just me and him alone. These are the deadliest of moments, standing alone before the big event begins. I stood and waited and waited, trying not to think about anything. The waiting is always worse than the doing.

I heard someone walking from far down the hall, and when I tried to look inside, I noticed their white screen door. It was just like the one we'd had in the house in Queens. I thought again, for the thousandth time, about that day as a child and the strangeness of seeing my father on the outside. Here I was now, in the present, but on the other side.

He opened the door but didn't smile. He looked healthy to me, or healthy enough, standing in his robe. His expression didn't change when he saw me. He too must have been sitting around in his own dreadful moments of waiting for me to arrive. I opened the screen door myself and stepped forward. I used to hug him when I visited, the kind of awkward one-sided hug you give to people who don't seem to know what to do. I didn't this time. He offered me a cold handshake, which I took. Then I stepped inside, and he followed behind me.

I hadn't been in the house in over a year, but it looked the same. It was a house built for making memories with grandchildren, for them to run across the floors chasing toys, and for family reunions on the deck overlooking green hills and tall trees. The house was quiet now. He walked me toward the living room, stopping near the kitchen to offer me something to drink. It was the same kitchen where he'd told me he didn't see why he should have to do any work. How far we've come since that day, I thought, given what I was about to ask him to talk about now.

He brought me a glass of water, and I sat on the couch across from his favorite chair. He went to get a blanket, telling me the chemotherapy had given him chills. He needed help to stay warm. He said it verbosely, as if he wanted me to respond or empathize, but I couldn't. I had nothing to offer. I felt empathy for him in the same way I'd feel for anyone who was sick, but not in the way I'd feel for someone close to me.

When I went to take out my notebook, there was a surprise. My hands weren't working. They shook, and this surprised me so much that I held up my hands to look at them, as if they belonged to someone else. I didn't want my father to notice, so I quickly put them on my knees to hide their secret. I felt calm, but my body knew how loaded this moment was and betrayed what it knew. There was a rush in my mind, a powerful energy of a presence I couldn't explain. "This is something that happens," I said to myself. Abandoned sons who interview their fathers. Men who have affairs. Families that are broken. Art that is made. I felt amazed all this was happening. I'd never have imagined this year for anyone in any family.

I suspected he'd be difficult, like a mob boss on a witness stand. That he'd deflect his way out of all but the most trivial of questions. Instead, my father seemed oddly pleased to be interviewed. I asked if I could record the interview on my phone, and he asked rhetorically, "You're going to record this, huh?", as if he was impressed. I wasn't sure if he was impressed with me for being so thorough, or proud that someone would want to record him. I struggled with the voice recorder on my iPhone to make sure it was recording, and my shaky hands didn't help. On the fifth try, it worked. As I began, he said, mostly to himself, "I've never been interviewed for a book before."

The first questions were about the facts of this new affair: who she was, how they met, how decisions were made. He seemed proud. It didn't seem to matter that he was talking to his son about it, which I didn't mind. This was his chance to say and be who he was, and that's what he did. I asked him whose idea it was to go to Australia, and he paused, aware suddenly that there was a moral boundary at stake. He smiled, perhaps to himself, and said that yes, it was his idea. He told me she hadn't wanted him to come since he was married, but he had convinced her. Despite all that had happened since that day, he was still proud he'd made it all happen.

I asked if he hadn't gotten sick what he would have done. He thought long and hard about this and eventually said it was "53/47," that he'd decided to leave my mother and go to Australia. It was odd to put a decision like this in numerical terms, as it meant all of us, my mother, my brother, his kids, and I, added up to forty-seven – close, but not enough compared to this new person in his life. But I don't believe he decided at all. He would have stayed in limbo for as long as my mother and his mistress let him. I think to him, in the present, it sounded better to have decided. It made him sound more sympathetic to himself. But since this was his reporting on his own memories, there is no way to know the truth.

Slowly, my questions worked their course, and as the hour went on, his games began. He told me at one point that during this year he'd been exiled from his family. That we had cast him out unfairly. That his therapist had told him he was a good parent. He said his oncologist was surprised that we hadn't rallied to his support. These were a form of bait, which I resisted. I took a moment to calmly correct him, in that his choosing to leave his family was not exile. We didn't force him to go to Australia. I don't think he understood the distinction. Somehow he believed, after everything he'd done, that he was owed far more than what he had been getting from us.

Toward the end, he lost his poise. He denied not staying in touch with me. He offered as proof that he had wanted to come visit Seattle but that I had "refused him." In frustration, he said that he couldn't see me any less than he had. This was enough for me. I stood up and said, "Really, you couldn't see me less?", suggesting I would head for the door. He asked why I was upset, but I knew he wouldn't understand. He was genuinely mystified as to why he'd been so isolated from his family. He couldn't see how he'd brought this onto himself.

I told him I was done, that he'd answered all of my questions. I had what I needed and was ready to leave. He became sweet. He suggested we take a break and that I might think of more questions later. Still standing, I said, "I don't see the point." I'd finally learned I didn't have to stay. His face fell silent and sad. Somehow he'd never imagined the interview would end this way. I told him, "You reap what you sow, Dad. And you need to plant some new seeds and start sowing." His sadness shifted to anger, and he repeated this back to me sarcastically, shaking his head. We walked to the door, and when I was outside, I turned to him. A part of me didn't want it to end this way, but we were out of alternatives. I told him I hope he feels better, shook his hand, and then walked away.

I got in the car and drove back to my brother's house, relieved beyond measure to be on my way home to family. I needed to bring stories of the past, lessons from my father and myself, to fill these voids so they didn't get passed on again. I told Jessica and Josh what I'd learned, and promised to share more with them through this book.

I haven't seen my father, or the ghosts I'd made of him, since that day. He and I will always be connected, but I can only hope he understands why I'm so far away.

ACKNOWLEDGEMENTS

My big brother Todd supported this project from the beginning. He read every draft and spent long hours with me comparing memories, sharing stories, and answering my questions. He helped me understand who I am, what family means, and how to tell this story.

Thanks to my mother Judi and my father Howard for letting me interview them for this book. I hope they both find happiness.

I'm grateful to Vanessa Longacre, Richard Grudman, and Heather Bussing for reading early drafts and for their feedback and honest conversations. Jill Stutzman gave feedback on a later draft, and of course, made the art project that inspired many important choices I've made in my life.

The book cover was designed by Tim Kordik, inspired by a photo taken by Teresa Brazen, with the actual cover photo by Christian Keller. I did the interior design based on the Balance template from BookDesignTemplates.com.

Thanks to copyeditors Emma Simmons and Karen Gill for polishing my prose. Kudos to proofreaders Amy Berkun, Eric Lawrence, Alyssa Fox, Vanessa Longacre and Emma Simmons. Honorary mention to my favorite escalope, Marlowe Shaeffer.

This book was funded by 247 backers on Kickstarter. Without them, this book might not exist. It made all the difference in the world while writing it to know they were interested in my story. Their names are listed below in the order of their pledge of support. Thanks to you all:

Ann Hudspeth, Lorelei Brown, Hillel Cooperman, Doug Shaw, Karen, David Fisher, Haider Al-Mosawi, Vernon Richards, Alice Merchant, Niklas Hall, Glenn Tanimura, Elisabeth Binder, Cornell Stamoran, Tara Becker, Sebastian Tecsi, Sam Greenfield, Tim Kwiatkowski, Greg Martinez, Christopher Kwan, Steve Ball, Jeffrey Bialy, Dimitris Georgakopoulos, Maria Kheyman, Norm Sun, Dave Wilson, Jenny Lam, Alyssa Fox, Todd Berkun, Matt Perry, Justin Esparza, Jon Whipple, Stefan Loble, Andrew McAdams, Shawn Murphy, Carolyn Monaco, Rachel Houghton, Matthew Freeman, Dominic Son, Doug Hanke, Ryan Sommers, Josh Rensch, Martin McClellan, Jason Copenhaver, Josh, Dan McComb, Jane Pyle, Kiran Umapathy, Dmitri Schoeman, Marla Erwin, Chris Kenst, Mary Prendiville, Elumar De Sa, Kevin Marsden, Dave Orkin, Martha Garvey, Heather Bussing, Nadja Haldimann, J. George, Geordie Korper, Mary Street, Mark Capaldi, Smaranda Calin, Ethan Cerami, Mark Ashley, Dan Brown, George B. Hopkins, Lisa Bailey, Micah Wilson, Richard Green, Justin Shreve, Denny Atkin, Robin Smail, Mike Ahn, Elliot, Paolo Malabuyo, Gina Trapani, ER, Kixhead, Chris Davis, Chris Winters, Sark Mahdasian, Diana, Dan Poineau, Niek Dewilde, Rod Robinson, Robert Fayle, Bryan Garwood, Audrey Nagel, Maarten Volders, Brian Fitzpatrick, Kwame Davis, Angela Wang, Mel Lafferty, Cosimo Streppone, Phillip Hunter, Adam Rice, Martin Page, Justin Adams, Marek Kowalkiewicz, Lane Becker, Justin Martenstein, Keith Bilbrey, Joe McCarthy, Eric Mann, P.Boman, Jason Mechler, Chris Brown, Toby Malina, Lauren Hall-Stigerts, Bryan Zug, Joan Shreve, Anne Williams, Brian Rasmussen, Craig Marl, Terrel Lefferts, Brad Wasserman, Marya Figueroa, Ruth Scott, Harold Strawbridge, Jorge Oliveira, Patrick Vlaskovits, Ron Perry, Sara Young, Steve Makofsky, Paul Walker, Brian Thurston, Gretchen Imbergamo, Juozas, Aaron Wroblewski, C.Y. Lee, Angel Ponce, Yvonne Seidl, Ario Jafarzadeh, Carol Gunby, Alex Koloskov, Jose Marques, Dan Ritz, Noah Fang, Daniel Lopez, Alan Page, Alan Leeds, Michael Earl, Eric Lawrence, Gayna Williams, Andraz Piletic, Jason Luther, Jen Matson, Shaji, Pavol Vaskovic, David Tate, Aimee Whitcroft, Florian Bugiel, Kitt Hodsden, Cgibernau, Nikolay Bachiyski, Mike Adams (mdawaffe), Kristoffer Andersson, Tom de Bruin, Gareth Marshall, Cynthia Lawson Jaramillo, JP, Ric Hayman, David W. Gray, Alberta Soranzo, Stepan Reznikov, Doug Mayo-Wells, Yoav Farhi, Jay Goldman, Dan Brodnitz, Clarissa Peterson, Stephen Arbour, Kris Arnold, Wayne Rambo, Unmesh Gundecha, Nick, Mark Norman Francis, Tom Burger, Larry Briggs, Ramon van der Weiden, Daniel Heinrich, Ravindra Gangadat, Chris Keppler, Steve Garfield, Anne Petersen, Juan Orozco, Kris Luyten, Adam Wygle, Dan Shapiro, Pablos, Zachary Cohn, Stuart Maxwell, Bill Smartt, Elisabeth Robson, Rob Staenke, Ellen Chisa, Leslie Gerhat, Mihai Costin, Daniel Escapa, Rachel, Heather, Nicole Steinbok, Byron Carr, Victor Lee, Charing, David Edery, Lee Cockrell, Jaree Wolfe, Nathan Lozeron, Andy Peatling, Leigh Reyes, Eric, Graham Haythornthwaite, Hana Kazazovic, Rob Irizarry, Lisa Phillips, George Valsamidis, Claude Emond, Filip Vandueren, Michael Susz, Lemar Hernandez, Betsy Aoki, Chris Wiegman, Faisal N. Jawdat, Seth Hein, Karen Bachmann, Dianne Por Supuesto, Alexandre Rocha Lima e Marcondes, Joe Horwood, and Mic Milic Frederick.

HOW YOU CAN HELP THIS BOOK

If this book was meaningful to you, please help it find its way in the world. It won't take more than a minute.

Please do two things right now:

1. **Write a review** of the book on Amazon.com. It's the simplest way to share your opinions of the book to influence others. This link will take you right there:

   http://bit.ly/ghostofmyfather-k

2. **Join my mailing list**. If you liked this book, joining this list is the best way to get news about related projects, announcements of new works and early notice of when I'll be on tour near you. You'll get a free sampler pack with chapters from all my books just for signing up:

   http://scottberkun.com/follow

Thank you.

SUPPORT BIG BROTHERS BIG SISTERS OF AMERICA

Half of all profits from this edition of this book will be donated to Big Brothers Big Sisters of Puget Sound and Big Brothers Big Sisters of America.

In exploring my own story I discovered this organization is a great way to help children in need of positive adult role models to get the mentoring and support they need. It can change young lives for the better, much like my big brother and other adults outside of my family changed mine.

Please consider donating your time, resources, or support to your nearest chapter, which you can find here: http://www.bbbs.org/.

Right now, thousands of children who need positive mentors are waiting, as the demand far outweighs the supply of people willing to help.

ABOUT THE AUTHOR

Scott Berkun is the best-selling author of *The Myths of Innovation, Confessions of a Public Speaker, Mindfire: Big Ideas for Curious Minds*, and *The Year Without Pants*. His work as a writer and public speaker has appeared in the *Washington Post, New York Times, Wired Magazine, Fast Company, Forbes Magazine*, and other media. He has taught creative thinking at the University of Washington and has been a regular commentator on CNBC, MSNBC, and National Public Radio. His popular essays and entertaining lectures are free at www.scottberkun.com, where you can sign up for a monthly email of all his recent and best work. He tweets at @berkun.

COLOPHON

Book cover designed by Tim Kordik
Cover font: Gotham, Gotham Light
Interior book design based on the Balance template from BookDesignTemplates.com
Heading font: Candal
Body text font: Rosarivo
Metaphors: recycled and customized AA rated
Caliber: .99
Joke: Why did the family cross the road?
Toad: Yellow
Paradox: paradox